INSIGHTS INTO ISLAMIC HUMANISM
A Comprehensive Approach

INSIGHTS INTO ISLAMIC HUMANISM

A Comprehensive Approach

by

Abdul Ali

MD Publications Pvt Ltd

New Delhi

Published by
MD Publications Pvt Ltd
"MD House" 11, Darya Ganj
New Delhi-110002
Tel. : +91-11-41563325, 41562846
Fax : +91-11-29235450
E-mail : contact@mdppl.com
Website : www.mdppl.com

ISBN : 978-81-904551-8-3

Price : Rs. 495/-

Published and Printed by **MD Publications Pvt Ltd** at Times Press, 910, Jatwara Street, Darya Ganj, New Delhi.

CONTENTS

Acknowledgements (vii)

Preface (ix)

1. **An Introduction to Western Distortions of Islam** 1
2. **Fundamental Principles of Islam : Humanistic Aspirations** 13
3. **Tolerance in Islam** 27
4. **The Status of Women in Islam** 47
5. **Humanistic Aspects of Conditional Polygamy in Islam** 61
6. **Islamic Approach to Abolition of Slavery** 71
7. **Treatment of Animals in Islam** 85
8. **Islam and Science** 93
9. **Arab-Islamic Legacy to Humour Literature** 129
10. **Islam : The Concept of Punishment** 161
11. **Legitimacy of Fresh Judgement in Islam** 169
12. **Secular Dimensions of Islam for Peaceful Co-existence in Pluralistic Societies** 181

Bibliography

Index

ACKNOWLEDGEMENTS

Some chapters of this book are based on my research paper's published in different journals of international repute. They are reproduced here with suitable emendations and additions. I am thankful to the editorial bodies of the journals—*Hamdard Islamics*, Pakistan; *The Muslim World League Journal*, Saudi Arabia; and *Islamic Culture*, India-for publishing the articles. I should like also to express my gratefulness to the various authors, references to whose works have been cited in the book. My thanks are also due to Mr. Kabir Ahmad Khan, Assistant Librarian, the Institute of Islamic Studies, Aligarh Muslim University, Aligarh, for giving me the benefit of his masterly location of books.

Finally, I wish to thank Messrs MD Publications, New Delhi, for undertaking publication of this volume.

May 2007 **Abdul Ali**

PREFACE

It is sad to note that Islam which contributed a great deal to human thought and progress during the early years of its history remains a misunderstood and misrepresented religion not only by non-Muslims, but also by such Muslims themselves who consider framing fresh laws in the context of the modern socio-economic and political developments as an unpardonable act of blasphemy. They have also ceased to be representative ambassadors of their religion to the outside world.

On the one hand, it is generally contended by non-Muslim writers on Islam that lasting peace and co-operation between Muslims and non-Muslims is not possible as the former are under religious obligation to carry on the holy war against the latter for the purpose of compelling them to accept the Muslim faith. Besides, judging from the deplorable educational and economic conditions of the present-day Muslims, they tend to consider it as outmoded and antagonistic to human development. They also look upon it as a symbol of backwardness and primitive barbarism.

Furthermore, being ignorant of the moral, spiritual and humanistic values of Islam, they deride its teachings and belittle its importance as a civilizing factor. While seeking to support their viewpoints, they hold that the system which approves of slavery, degrades the position of women in society, encourages polygamy, provides for the holy war for the purpose of proselytization, prescribes such punishments as stoning to death, mutilation, whippings etc., is not only obsolete and antiquated, but also contrary to all norms of human behaviour.

It is worthy of mention in this context that the mistrust about Islam in the West is deep-rooted in history. It is common knowledge that ever since the Middle Ages when Muslims drove Christian crusaders out of Asia, Western poets, writers, and scholars like Dante, Gibbon, Waltaire, etc. had painted Prophet Muhammad in the blackest of colours. They ridiculed his teachings and described his followers as barbarians. They misrepresented Muslims as savage conquerors who carried fire and sword wherever they went and as vandals who destroyed palaces, churches and temples, and burnt down libraries. In spite of the fact that the crusades came to an end long-long ago, the grave distortions and misrepresentations to which Islam was subjected by the West, continue to be propagated and highlighted by Western media with added fury and vehemence even today.

On the other hand, there has been no dearth of religious bigots among the Muslims who have miserably failed in their perception of the spirit of Islam. They are found more concerned with petty matters relating to outward manifestations of the religion than with piety itself, cultivation of which among its followers is the immediate and ultimate objective of Islam. They are not only unacquainted with the broad humanistic stands taken by this religion in tackling various socio-economic and political problems faced by man, but also appear to be unaware of the very conception of worship in Islam. That is the main reason why lethargy has taken the place of dynamism in their life and they are found lagging far behind developed nations of the world in science, technology and other branches of knowledge and learning. In short, they have stifled the spirit of Islam in its outward manifestations. In the present work an attempt has been made to assess the contribution of Islam as a civilizing agency with special reference to its broad secular, liberal and humanistic aspects in a manner that enables modern minds to comprehend and appreciate them fully.

ABDUL ALI

1

AN INTRODUCTION TO WESTERN DISTORTIONS OF ISLAM

Misconceptions about Islam in the West are galore. They are perpetrated mostly by Jewish and Christian writers. The mistrust about Islam is not the result of independent thinking of the Western people, but rather it is closely related with their age-old hostile attitude towards this religion and its followers. This hostility, generated mainly by the triumph of Islam over Judaism and Christianity in the Middle Ages, seems to have been a powerful factor in determining the Western attitude towards it. As is well-known, the successors of Prophet Muhammad conquered Christianity in Hira, Yemen, Syria, Egypt and Constantinople. The fight continued for several centuries between Christendom and Islam. The war was not limited to swords and weapons alone. It spread out to the fields of debate and controversy also. This gave birth to a large number of Orientalists who produced a vast body of literature on Islam which is replete with grave and mischievous inaccuracies. Since Islam still remains the most formidable and potential rival to the modern West, their hostility is reflected in countless ways even now.[1]

By and large until the mid-eighteenth century, Orientalists were Biblical scholars who wrote with the missionary zeal to distort the image of Islam by their unfair criticism of the Islamic way of life. They painted Prophet Muhammad in the blackest of colours, and ridiculed his teachings. They described Muslims as savage conquerors who carried fire and swords, wherever they went. They also charged them with having destroyed palaces, churches, temples as well as burnt down libraries. They presented Islam as outmoded and antagonistic to the scientific development of man by attacking the very lofty solutions which it offered to the sufferings of humanity in all spheres of life, for which it should rather have been appreciated by them. In this way, they invented and perpetuated false notions about Islam and Muslims in an organised way, and produced a large number of books in condemnation of Islamic tenets. It is estimated that around 60,000 books, dealing with the Near Orient were written by Orientalists between 1800 and 1950 while the number of Oriental books produced in the East about the West is quite negligible.[2]

If we go through the works of the orientalists, it appears that, barring a few exceptions, like Godfrey Higgins, Thomas Carlyle, John Davenport, Lamartine, etc. the majority of them wrote on Islam with the sole objective of refuting the concept of the divine origin of this religion as well as representing Prophet Muhammad as a scheming impostor, a falsehood incarnate. They looked upon Islam as a symbol of barbarism and a religion of sensuality. They supported this point by telling that the Prophet permitted polygamy, and he himself had a great many wives. "What an idea of Islam ! But it is the idea in the minds of ninety-nine out of one hundred Britishers."[3]

The critics further argued that the Prophet, far from being divinely inspired, was predominantly dependent upon Jewish and Christian sources in the formulation of his doctrines. For example, C. C. Torrey in his book *The Jewish Foundation of Islam* asserted that the Prophet was a disciple of the synagogue, while W. Ahrens maintained that the Christian influences were decisive for him.[4] They further held that Islam, by its immutable dogmas, paralysed the brain and killed all initiative. Consider the following statement given by Andre Servier in support of this point in his book *Islam and the Psychology of the Musulman*:

> How is it that the Syrians, the Egyptians, the Berbers, as soon as they became Islamised, lost the energy, the intelligence and the spirit of initiative they exhibited under the domination of Greece and Rome? How has it come about that the Arabs themselves who, according to the historians, were the professors of science and philosophy in the West, can have forgotten all their brilliant accomplishments and have sunk into a state of ignorance that today relegates them to the barbarous nations ?[5]

In order to be acquainted with the true nature of Orientalism, a passing reference to a few eminent Orientalists would not be out of place here. In his *Weltgeschichte* (1881-1888), Ranke sought to expose the inferiority of Islam by speaking of it as defeated by the Germanic-Romanic peoples ; and in his *Historische Fragmente*, Burckhardt condemned it as wretched and trivial, while Noldeke declared in 1887 that his main objective as an Orientalist had been to confirm his low opinion of the Eastern peoples.[6]

Similarly, Ignaz Goldziher, though he appreciated the tolerance of Islam towards other religions, bitterly criticised what is called Muhammad's anthropomorphism ; Duncan Black Macdonald considered Islam as heretical Christianity ; Carl Becker looked upon Islamic civilization as a sadly undeveloped one ; C. Snouck Hurgronji's studies of Islamic mysticism made him critical of its limitations ; while Louis Massignon remained critical of Islam for its rejection of the idea of incarnation. As described by Edward W. Said, the above five scholars were the architects of the image of Islam in the West in the late nineteenth and early twentieth century.[7]

The twentieth century Orientalists fared no better than their predecessors. They never tired of subjecting the tenets of Islam to biased criticism. They attributed the overall backwardness of the present-day Muslims to what they regarded as the element of anti-humanism in Islamic civilization by depicting Islam as the enemy of scientific thought and progress. For instance, Wollaston in 1905, Lammens in 1926, Anderson and Watt in the 1960s, only reiterated the baseless assumption that the Quran was the result of wishful thinking and that it could have been written by any Arab who is acquainted with the general outline of the Jewish history and of the traditions of his own country and possessed some poetic fire and fancy.[8]

Some of the critics have gone to the extremes of indecent behaviour in dealing with the Prophet. They did not spare even his person and attributed to him the most unbecoming and slanderous names. This is clear from the following statement made by Maxime Rodinson :

"We know very little for certain about this man whose ideas and actions have shaken the world, but, as with Jesus, we may get through the unreliable tales and one-sided traditions, a glimpse of something that is the echo of a remarkable personality which astonished the ordinary men who gathered around it. It is this echo as I believe I have glimpsed it, that I have tried to capture in this book. The picture is not a simple one. It is neither the satanic monster of some nor the best of all created things of others, neither the cold-blooded impostor nor the political theorist, nor the mystic wholly in love with God. If we have understood him rightly, Mohammad was a complex man, full of contradictions." He was fond of his pleasures, yet indulged in bouts of asceticism. He was often compassionate, yet sometimes cruel. He was a believer consumed with the love and fear of God, and a politician ready for any expedient. Without any gift of eloquence in ordinary life, he was able for a short period to produce, from his unconscious, phrases of disturbing poetic quality. He was cool and nervous, brave and timid, a mixture of cunning and frankness, forgiving and at the same time capable of terrible vindictiveness, proud and humble, chaste and sensual, intelligent and, in certain things, oddly stupid. But there was a power in him which, with the help of circumstances, was to make him one of the rare men who have turned the world upside down."[9]

Besides, even better informed enlightened Western historians are not only found sunk in depths of ignorance in regard to the dynamism and humanistic aspects of Islam, but also have consistently and deliberately played down its contribution to human thought and progress. While recording the story of civilization, they usually jump from the Greeks to the Renaissance in total neglect of the contribution made by the Arabs and Muslims in the development of science. Bernal's book *Science in History*, in four volumes of 1325 pages, is an example of this pattern, in which the author has devoted only 10 pages to Islamic science.[10]

Again, C.E.M. Joad, author of *The Story of Civilization* while talking of the contribution of religion to the advancement of human civilization, did not include Prophet Muhammad among the great religious teachers chosen by him. Emphasizing the civilizing importance of the religious teachings of Buddha, Lao-Tse, Confucius and Jesus Christ, he says:

> "If men lived the kind of life which these four great religious teachers urged them to live, the world would be much better and happier, and at the same time a more civilized place than it is or ever has been."[11]

It is indeed surprising that the author has not given even a passing reference to the great role played by the Prophet and his followers in advancing the cause of knowledge and learning. On the contrary, he has dismissed the Arab caliphs and rulers as uncivilized. Interestingly enough, his chief source of information about them was the Arabian Nights. To quote his own words :

> "But in the main the princes and the princesses, the caliphs whom you meet in the Arabian Nights, and the rich and powerful of all countries, were content, as most people have always been content to get what they liked and to enjoy it. At bottom most of these kings and rulers were just treacle toffee eaters. So the Empires and the caliphs and the kings and princes don't for the most part come into this book."[12]

Similarly, the biased Orientalists never tired of charging Islam with being militant and intolerant towards members of other religions. They held the view that the savage nomadic Arab tribes spread the Islamic religion by the sword and flame between the seventh and ninth centuries. Dr. S. Margoliouth has highlighted this charge in the following words :

> "Towards the end of the Prophet's career, an injunction is given quite in accordance with Noah's prayer: When the sacred months are ended, slay the associators wheresoever ye find them. When ye meet those that disbelieve, behead them, until ye have made a massacre of them, and then make fast their bonds ; after which be gracious or take ransom. In accordance with this order the Islamic system recognised two communities as having the right to exist : the Muslims, who were to be dominant, and the People of the Book, who were to be subjugated ; all others were to be exterminated."[13]

From what precedes, it is sufficiently clear that Islam is fundamental by misrepresented in the West, and through it all over the world. The above-mentioned Edward W. Said, a

Palestinian scholar, has in his book *Orientalism* very successfully exposed the fallacies of the Orientalists. It is undoubtedly a scholarly work. He has given a very brilliant and far-reaching critique of the attitudes that the West has traditionally assumed towards the East. He is perfectly right when, he says that Western anti-Semitism and Orientalism resemble each other very closely. He further denounced such Orientalists by saying that "they are not academics, but beneficiaries of the academic study of the Orient."[14]

Now a few words regarding rebuttal of some of the main charges levelled by the biased critics against Islam would not be out of place here. Contrary to their accusations, Islam remains a scientific way of living which aims at both spiritual fulfillment and material well-being of man. It came to give him confidence in his own destiny by enlightening him both in relation to his Creator and the universe. He is described as master of the universe and the noblest creature. Everything in the universe is created to serve him. Even the angels are below him in rank and dignity. He is ordained to perform his role as benefactor of humanity by establishing and promoting on earth a highly civilized society based on the ethical framework of Islam for peaceful co-existence comprising tolerance, freedom of faith and conscience, universal brotherhood of mankind as well as principles of humanism.

Far from setting unattainable ideals for its followers, Islam is a practical and utilitarian religion in the sense that all its teachings of ethics and virtues, individual and public morality, its inspiration for cultivation of knowledge and learning, its political structure as well as its purely religious duties centring on the five pillars of Islam-i.e., the profession of faith, prayers, fasting, alms-giving and pilgrimage-they are all designed to promote human happiness and prosperity. It also gave a very comprehensive conception of worship which consists not only in prayers of its follower, but also in his active participation in exploring and pressing into the service of man all the seen and unseen forces and objects of nature for the welfare of humanity at large. As such all the actions and functions, efforts and endeavours made by man in this direction, right from going to bed for rest and sleep to sacrificing his life in the cause of justice and truth, are regarded as worship in Islam. No wonder, a true follower of Islam is simultaneously a benefactor of humanity as well as worshipper of God.

Secular and tolerant, the political spirit of Islam is another great contribution of this religion to the advancement of human civilization. It is common knowledge that lack of tolerance and courtesy on the part of one religious community towards another often triggers off communal disturbances that threaten the very stability of society. But Islam has struck at the very root of this problem by making it binding up its followers to develop a tolerant and secular attitude towards members of other religions. One chief feature of Islamic tolerance is that it constitutes an essential part of this religion, as it is strictly enjoined in a number of Quranic verses and Traditions of Prophet Muhammad. They not only prohibit Muslims from imposing their faith on non-Muslims, but also exhort them to treat the latter gently and leniently. They are also enjoined to practice utmost restraint, endurance and patience in their treatment of non-Muslims as well as to respect their prophets and religious authorities.

It is worthy of mention in this context that Prophet Muhammad himself meted out a very kind and generous treatment to non-Muslims not only in the early years of his prophethood, but also in the later years when he was at the height of his power and at the head of a large army. Numerous instances can be quoted in support of this point. Here it will suffice to mention that the way he treated the delegation of the Christians of Najran has no parallel in the history of other conquerors. He not only played host to them and lodged them in the Prophetic Mosque, but also permitted them to offer prayers on Christian lines in the same Mosque. Perhaps, a similar example of secularism is hard to find elsewhere.[15]

In order to keep Islam modern and progressive in every age there is the provision of *ijtihad* (original thinking and independent judgment) for framing fresh laws to satisfy new conditions in accordance with the spirit of Islam. This keeps the evolutionary spirit of Muslim jurisprudence alive as well as authorises its followers to legislate for themselves to meet their modern requirements. Thus, the doors of *ijtihad* are as wide open today as they might have been in the times of Prophet Muhammad and his immediate successors.

Likewise, the Orientalists' charge regarding polygamy which is described by them as one of the chief offences of Islam against the fair sex, is based on their negative attitude towards this religion. It is true that Islam did not reject polygamy outright, but it never encouraged it nor did it make it binding upon its followers. It is conveniently overlooked by the critics that the humanised form of polygamy as retained by Islam is more of a social responsibility on the part of the polygamous Muslim male than of a means to enjoy the luxury of plurality of wives. The example of Prophet Muhammad himself is a sufficient proof in support of this point. Till the age of fifty-two he had only one wife, Khadijah, who was fifteen years senior to him. After her death he contracted a number of marriages. Except for Aishah all his wives were widows. He married them with a view to providing them with a home and a position they could not otherwise enjoy. For instance, Umme Salma had a number of children when her husband died in the battle of Uhud. It was only out of sympathy for her as well as in recognition of the sacrifices made by her husband that the Prophet married her. His remaining marriages were also motivated by similar considerations. This shows that by being polygamous he was not satisfying his lust but acting as a reformer.

Lastly, as regards Islam's contribution to the scientific and intellectual development of man only a passing reference to it can be attempted here. Inspired by Quranic verses and Apostolic Traditions, the Muslims were filled with the spirit of scientific inquiry. They soon developed a keen sense of intellectual curiosity and a voracious appetite for learning. They travelled far and wide in search of knowledge and contributed a great deal to human thought and progress by pursuing and patronising study and research in all branches of learning. For example, Ibn Khaldun, the founder of the modern sciences of sociology and historiography, was the greatest historical thinker of Islam. In the field of geography the names of Ibn Khurdadhbih, Ibn Hawqal, Yaqut, Al-Bakri and Al-Idrisi are very famous. The great mathematician, Al-Khawarizmi, wrote the oldest work on algebra known as *Hisab-ul-Jabr w-al-Muqabalah* (the calculation of integration and equation), the Latin version of which was used until the sixteenth century as the main mathematical text-book by Western scholars.[16] Likewise, their contributions to philosophical studies can be judged from the fact that Muslim philosophy continued to be taught in the universities of Europe up to the middle of the seventeenth century, and that Aristotle was understood in the West only through the commentaries of Ibn Rushd for a long time.[17]

Besides, the Muslims achieved considerable distinctions in Chemistry, Mineralogy, Oceanography, Botany, Fine Arts, Music, etc. Their contributions to these fields of study form the connecting link between the Greco-Roman classical age and modern civilization. In view of this fact the Muslims can justifiably claim to be harbingers of the modern scientific era.

In summing up, it may fairly be said that the charges and accusations levelled by the Western writers against Islam are totally unfounded and baseless. In striking contrast with their perceptions and distortions, Islam as an educational force not only inspired Muslims to cultivate knowledge and learning, but also infused in them the spirit of scientific inquiry which is the very life and soul of modern sciences. It may further be added that their lofty achievements in different branches of knowledge are the result of their having been closer to the spirit of Islam. It is, therefore, absolutely baseless to blame Islamic teachings for the current intellectual and educational decay of Muslims all over the world. Their backwardness in modern times can be best interpreted only in terms of their degeneration as followers of Islam. The moment they come closer to the spirit of Islam there is no reason why they cannot resume the heroic role played by them during the Middle Ages as benefactors of humanity as well as bearers of the torch of culture and civilization.

References

1. Maryam Jameelah, *Islam Versus Ahl Al-Kitab,* Delhi, 1982, p. xviii.

2. Edward W. Said, *Orientalism,* London, 1978, p. 204.

3. Lord Headley, *A Western Awakening to Islam,* London, 1914, p. 11.

4. Marlin L. Swartz (Ed.) *Studies on Islam,* Oxford University Press, 1981, p. 87.

5. Andre Servier, *Islam and the Psychology of the Musulman* (English translation), pp. 2-5.

6. Edward, We Said, *op.cit.,* pp. 208-209.

7. *Ibid.,* pp. 209.

6. Mohammed Khalifa, *The Sublime Qur'an and Orientalism,* New York, 1983, pp. 10-11.

9. Maxime Rodinson, *Mohammed* (tr. by Anne Carter), London, 1968, p. 313.

10. Mahmoud Dhaudi: "Contemporary Civilization's Crisis and Islamic Ethical Principles of Science" in *Islam Today*, No. 1, Morocco, p. 37.

11. C.E.M. Joad, *The Story of Civilization*, London, 1946, p. 29.

12. *Ibid.*, pp. 15.

13. D.S. Margoliouh, *Mohammed and the Rise of Islam*, London, 1906, pp. 86-87.

14. Edward W. Said, *op.cit.*, p. 223.

15. Shibli Nu'mani, *Sirat al-Nabi*, Vol. I, p. 292.

16. P.K. Hitti, *History of the Arabs*, p. 379.

17. 'Umar al-Dasuqi, *Fi al-Adab al-Hadith*, Vol. I, p. 470.

2

FUNDAMENTAL PRINCIPLES OF ISLAM : HUMANISTIC ASPIRATIONS

The mission of Prophet Muhammad was to proclaim the unity of Allah and the unity of man as well as to guide mankind to the path of virtue and righteousness. Islam, which means submission to the Will of Allah, is preeminently a practical religion. It offers no unattainable ideal. It came to give man confidence in his own destiny. It made clear that man was created to worship Allah and act as His vicegerent on earth. Everything else was created to serve him.

The second fundamental message which the Prophet gave to mankind was that man is born sinless and uninhibited by any past sins or blemish upon his conscience. It is the deeds of his lifetime that either tarnish his conscience and make him the very embodiment of evil or reward him both in the world and in the hereafter. He is not to be haunted by shadows of any sins committed in any past life, nor is he the inheritor of a sin committed by any remote ancestor. Thus, Islam gave a clean slate to man. It is for him to fashion his life according to his will and to make or mar his destiny.[1]

The third fundamental principle preached by the Prophet was the unity of mankind. Islam enjoins that mankind is a brotherhood and that there is no race on earth which did not have its prophets. The Muslims are required to believe in all the prophets and the scriptures revealed to them. Allah says: "The messenger believeth in that which hath been revealed unto him from his Lord and so do the believers. Each one believeth in Allah and His angels and His scriptures and His messengers—We make no distinction between any of His messengers-and they say: We hear, and we obey. (Grant us) Thy forgiveness, our Lord. Unto Thee is the journeying. (11:285). And again: Verily We have sent thee with the Truth, a comforter and warner; and there is not a people but a warner hath passed among them." (XXXV:24).

Another distinctive feature of Islam is that it established a direct relationship between man and his Creator. It abolished the ecclesiastical and priestly class who, posing as guardians of the faith, pretended to possess supernatural power. They exploited and persecuted their frightened followers by terrorising them into believing that mere confession to priests or receipt of chits of good conduct from them could serve as passports to paradise. Islam declared that the door of the Lord is ever open to every striver after Him. The Qur'an says: "Those who strive after Us, We show them Our way". "And when My servants ask you concerning Me, then surely I am near; I answer the prayer of the suppliant when he calls on Me, so they should answer My call and believe in Me, that they may find the right way". According to Islam, a prophet is a teacher, a guide and an exemplar, but he is not an intermediary. The belief in the intermediary is a remnant of paganism which weakens man's sense of responsibility and destroys his selfreliance. This belief crept into almost all the branches of theism from the beginning. It was not only the founder of a religion that was accepted as an intermediary between his people and Allah, but every man of known piety and righteousness after the founder was accepted as an intermediary. For example, Christ is not the only intermediary in Christendom, but after him Mary, Peter, Popes, Cardinals, even the ordinary priest, play the same role.[2] But the Prophet of Arabia abolished this system and relieved the world from the pernicious institution of socerdotalism. Lord Headley has acknowledged this great contribution of Islam to humanity in the following words:

"The advent of Mahomet, some six hundred years after Christ, exposed the unreality of all such ideas as atonements, priestly interventions, supplications to the saints, and those other cumbersome and involved methods of approaching the Almighty. However grand the Mosaic laws, however beautiful the gentle and forgiving precepts of the Holy Prophet of Nazareth, it must be admitted that the Mahomedan teaching contained the most sublime message, over-riding by its very simplicity all obstacles in the way of the believer on his path to God... Indeed, it is surprising that human beings with brains and intelligence should have been so foolish as to allow dogmas and the tricks of socerdotalism to obscure their view of Heaven and their Almighty Father, Who is always approachable by each one of His creatures, whether human or saintly (i.e., divinely inspired). The key to heaven is always there, and can be turned by the humblest or most miserable human being without any help from prophet, priest, or king. It is like the blessed air we breathe, free to all God's creatures, and those who try to make mankind think otherwise are probably guided by interested motives, e.g., salaries and stipends, which keep professions going, or some other worldly advantages".[3]

Another fundamental principle of Islam as preached by the Quran and the Prophet is the belief in life after death. After death man will be resurrected and judged on the basis of his deeds done in this worldly life. He shall be rewarded for good deeds and punished for bad actions. Thus, the earthly life is not an end in itself, but it is a transitory stage to a higher, fuller and abiding existence. This doctrine has a tremendous instrumental value. It tends to discipline man and develop in him a sense of accountability for his actions and behaviour in this life. While hope of the reward of eternal bliss in Paradise gives him the incentive to become virtuous, law-abiding, pious and God-fearing, fear of terrible agony in Hell makes him abstain from vices and evil deeds in this worldly life. The Day of Resurrection and Reckoning are repeatedly described in the Quran as mentioned below:

"When Earth is shaken with her (final) earthquake

And Earth yieldeth up her burdens,

And man saith: What aileth her?

That day she will relate her chronicles,

Because thy Lord inspireth her.

That day mankind will issue forth in scattered groups to be shown their deeds.

And whoso doeth good an atom's weight will see it then,

And whoso doeth ill an atom's weight will see it then".[4]

"The Calamity

What is the Calamity?

Ah, what will convey unto thee what the Calamity is

A day wherein mankind will be as thickly-scattered moths

And the mountains will become as carded wool.

Then, as for him whose scales are heavy (with good works),

He will live a pleasant life.

But as for him whose scales are light,

The Bereft and Hungry One will be his mother.

Ah, what will convey unto thee what she is-Raging fire".[5]

Pillars of Islam

Islam is the religion of submission to the Will of Allah. It seeks to realise this objective by prescribing certain devotional and religious practices for man which carry innumerable spiritual, moral and material benefits for him. His religious duties centre on the five pillars of Islam. "Worship is the pillar of religion", is one of the sayings of Prophet Muhammad. But the concept of worship has a very wide range in Islam. Allah Himself does not need man's worship of Him for His glorification. He is the Absolute, the Owner of Praise. The religious duties which He has prescribed for man are for his benefits alone. The real purpose behind them must be grasped and implemented by the worshipper in his day-to-day life. Worship must inspire him to inculcate virtues by preventing him from lewdness and iniquity. There is no place for empty prayers and rituals in Islam. The Quran itself does not make any allowance for such worshippers who fail to model their practical life on the message and teachings of the prayers. On the contrary, it has condemned them in the following words:

"Ah, woe unto worshippers

Who are heedless of their prayer;

Who would be seen (at worship)

Yet refuse small kindnesses."[6]

Likewise, Dr. Muhammad Iqbal has rightly criticised the hollowness and futility of the degraded form of prayer in the following words:

"Qawm kiya cheez hai qawmon ki imamat kiya hai,

Isko kiya jane ye bechare do rak'at ke Imam".

(What is meant by *ummah* (the Muslim community) and its leadership is beyond the comprehension of the poor Imam (the Muslim religious leader) offering a few genuflections of prayer).

That real piety or worship has a much deeper base than mere observance of rituals is described in the Quran as follows:

"It is not righteousness that ye turn your faces to the East and the West; but righteous is he who believeth in Allah and the Last Day and giveth his wealth, for love of Him, to kinsfolk and to orphans and the needy and the wayfarer and to those who ask, and to set slaves free; and observeth proper worship and payeth the poor-due. And those who keep their treaty when they make one, and the patient in tribulation and adversity and time of stress. Such are they who are sincere. Such are the God-fearing".[7]

Furthermore, Islam came to give man confidence in his own destiny by freeing his mind from the shackles of superstitions. It gave him the status of being the noblest creature of Allah. He is also made master of the universe. Everything else is created to serve him. Even the angels are below him in rank and dignity. Islam taught man to play the role of man rather than that of the angels on earth. Some of the Quranic verses describing the special blessings of Allah on man are quoted below:

> "Verily We have honoured the children of Adam. We carry them on the land and the sea, and have made provision of good things for them, and have preferred them above many of those whom We created with a marked preferment". (XVII:70)

> "He created the heavens and the earth with truth, and He shaped you and made good your shapes, and unto Him is the journeying", (LXIV: 3)

> "See ye not how Allah hath made serviceable unto you whatsoever is in the skies and whatsoever is in the earth and hath loaded you with His favours both without and within?" (XXXI: 20)

As regards the mission of man, it is vicegerancy of Allah on earth. He is asked to perform this role by establishing and promoting here a civilization based on high moral standards as well as on the principles of truth, justice and universal brotherhood of mankind. It is significant to note that all the actions and functions, efforts and endeavours made by him in this connection, right from going to bed for rest and sleep to sacrificing his life in the cause of justice, are regarded as worship in Islam. No wonder, a true follower of Islam is a 24-hour worshipper of Allah. It is only in the light of this fact that the following Quranic verse can be properly understood and appreciated:

> "I created the jinn and humankind only that they might worship Me. I seek no livelihood from them, nor do I ask that they should feed Me". (LI: 56-57)

Another important point which deserves to be mentioned in this regard is that moderation is the very backbone of Islamic worship. It is a virtue between two undesirable extremes. The Quran has advocated moderation in all matters and praised the Muslims as a moderate community. This is clear from the following verses:

> And thou (Muhammad), be not loud voiced in thy worship nor yet silent therein, but follow a way between". (XVII:110)

> "And let not thy hand be chained to thy neck nor open it with a complete opening, lest thou sit down rebuked, denuded". (XVII:29)

> "Thus We have appointed you a middle nation, that ye may be witnesses against mankind, and that the messenger may be a witness against you...[11] (11:143)

Doing good to humanity and making peace between one another are better acts of worship than mere fasting, giving out alms and saying prayers. Prophet Muhammad has summed up the spirit of real worship in the following words:

"Shall I not inform you of a better act than fasting, alms and prayers? Making peace between one another : enmity and malice tear up heavenly rewards by the roots".

In this way Islam gave a most comprehensive concept of worship which consists not only in prayers of the Muslim, but also in his active participation in exploring and pressing into the service of man all the seen and unseen forces and objects of Nature for the welfare of humanity at large.

Faith (*shahadah*) is the first pillar of Islam. It is summed up in the formula that there is no god but Allah, and that Muhammad is the Messenger of Allah.

Prayers five times a day at their appointed hours constitute the second pillar of Islam. These prayers that are made obligatory for the Muslim have both mundane and spiritual advantages. They enable the believers to meet one another five times a day on terms of perfect equality. Kings and slaves, masters and servants, rich and poor, blacks and whites, all forget their social status and racial differences, stand together rubbing shoulders with one another as equal brethren, and humble themselves before Almighty Allah. They also serve to regulate their life and keep them active, cheerful and healthy. The spiritual significance of the prayers has been vividly described by Shah Waliullah of Delhi as follows:

> "Know that one is sometimes transported, quick as lightning, to the Holy Precincts (of the Divine Presence), and finds one's self attached, with the greatest possible adherence, to the threshold of God. There descend on this person the Divine transfigurations (*tajalli*) which dominate his soul. He sees and feels things which the human tongue is incapable of describing. Once this state of light passes away, he returns to his previous condition, and finds himself tormented by the loss of such an ecstasy. Thereupon he tries to regain that which has escaped him, and adopts the condition of this lowly world which would be nearest to a state of absorption in the knowledge of the Creator. This is a posture of respect, of devotion, and of an almost direct conversation with God, which posture is accompanied by appropriate words and acts. Worship consists essentially of three elements: (1) humility of heart consequent on a feeling of the

presence of the majesty and grandeur of God, (2) recognition of this superiority (of God) and humbleness of man by means of appropriate words, and (3) adoption by the organs of the body, of postures of necessary reverence. To show our honour to somebody we stand up, with a fulsome concentration of attention, turning our faces towards him. Even more respectful is the state when we bend and bow our heads in reverence. Still greater respect is displayed by laying down the face-which reflects in the highest degree one's ego and self-consciousness so low that it touches the ground in front of the object of reverence. As a man can reach the top of his spiritual evolution only gradually, it is evident that such an ascension must pass through all the three stages; and a perfect service of worship would have three postures, Standing up, Bowing down, and Prostrating by laying the head on the ground in the presence of the Almighty; and all this is performed for the necessary evolution of the spirit, so that one might feel truly the sublimity of God and the humbleness of man".[8]

Payment of *zakat* (the poor-tax) is the third pillar of the faith. It is considered almost identical with piety. It is not a voluntary act of charity, but an obligatory tax on property, including money, cattle, corn, fruit and merchandise. In the Quran it is often associated with the prayer. The Prophet declared that *zakat* was a religious duty and a Divine prescription, on par with belief in one God, the service of prayers, fasting and Haj. If belief is a spiritual duty, and prayer, fasting and Haj are bodily duties, the payment of *zakat* is a fiscal duty. The main advantage of this provision is that it has proved to be an effective means for keeping wealth in constant circulation, for preventing its concentration in the hands of a chosen few. It also serves to improve the lot of the down-trodden and have-nots.

The next obligatory duty which every Muslim is required to perform is that of fasting during the month of Ramadan, the ninth month of the Muslim year. It is of special significance in the life of the Muslims because of the numerous spiritual benefits and temporal advantages attached to it. The word Ramadan is derived from 'Ramd' which in Arabic means "to burn". And the month is so called because fasting during it is supposed to burn away the sins and baser urges of man. It is for achieving this noble objective that fast during it is prescribed to every Muslim, both male and female. He is required to abstain from all food and drink from dawn till sunset throughout this month. The Quran speaks about it as follows:

> "The month of Ramadan in which was revealed the Quran, a guidance for mankind, and clear proofs of the guidance, and the Criterion (of right and wrong). And whosoever of you is present, let him fast the month, and whosoever of you is sick or on a journey, (let him fast the same) number of other days. Allah desireth for you ease; He desireth not hardship for you; and (He desireth) that ye should complete the period, and that ye should magnify Allah for having guided you, and that peradventure ye may be thankful."[9]

Obviously, the fast is a rigorous one, particularly in the summer season when the days are long and temperature goes high. Even a drop of water is not allowed to go down the throat to slake the thirst. Nevertheless, it is not beyond the capacity of the normal human being to perform it, because this is the prescription of Allah and Allah does not task a soul beyond its capacity as mentioned in the Quran. The religious life of the Muslim remains very busy during this month. He becomes very particular in offering the prescribed prayers in the mosque five times a day, namely at the early morning, mid-day, after-noon, evening and night. Additional prayers are also offered after the night prayer. These are called *tarawih,* in which the whole Quran is recited at least once during the month in every mosque. In some mosques it is recited twice or thrice or even more, depending upon the capacity of the *hafiz* who leads the *tarawih* prayers. Besides, devout Muslims seclude themselves for some time in the mosque during this month, and abstain from all worldly conversation. This seclusion is known as *I'tikaf*. Prophet Muhammad used to observe this practice in the last ten days of the month.

Fasting during this month gives the Muslim a rigorous spiritual exercise which trains him in endurance, self-control as well as in fighting temptation of all kinds. It also helps him in gaining control over his *nafse-ammarah,* which is responsible for all the beastly and baser urges in him such as greed, jealousy, anger, lust for power, fornication, exploitation, usurping the rights of others and adopting corrupt means of acquiring worldly gains, etc. It also benefits in the matter of health, discipline and development of will-power. Besides, having realised for himself the pangs of hunger and thirst, the fasting Muslim becomes more charitably disposed towards his unfortunate brethren living below the poverty line. It is worth mentioning in this context that fasting should not be confused with hunger. It is more than that. It enjoins not only abstinence from eating and drinking, but also complete control of passions and carnal desires, in the absence of which fasting goes in vain and does not earn any credit or reward for the fasting Muslim. Two sayings of the Prophet are quoted below in this regard:

> "Whosoever does not abandon lying, falsehood and corrupt practices, Allah does not want him to abstain from his food and drink."

> "There are many keepers of fast who gain nothing by fasting but thirst, and there are many risers up at night and performers of prayers who gain nothing by their rising but wakefulness."

The *Hajj* or pilgrimage to the Sacred House of Allah in Mecca is the final pillar and one of the finest institutions of Islam. It is obligatory, at least once in a lifetime, upon every Muslim, both male and female, who is mentally, financially and physically fit.

Allah says:

> "Lo! the first Sanctuary appointed for mankind was that at Becce (Mecca), a blessed place, a guidance to the peoples; Wherein are plain memorials (of Allah's guidance); the place where Abraham stood up to pray; and whosoever entereth it is safe. And pilgrimage to the House is a duty unto Allah for mankind, for him who can find a way thither..."[10]

The *Hajj* is the largest annual convention of the faith, in which believers from all over the world assemble in all humility in response to the call of Allah. It gives them the opportunity to exchange views, to discuss their problems, and to promote their general welfare. Collectively, the greatest gain to the Muslim community is the spirit of universal brotherhood and equality which manifests itself through this institution. The process starts at the very moment when, upon arriving at the border of the sacred territory around Mecca, the pilgrims put off their normal dress and put on the *ihram* (a seamless dress prescribed for the *Hajj*). This single act ends all difference in dress. All of them, kings and beggars, rich and poor, are reduced to the same status. This dress demonstrably obliterates all marks of distinctions. As such it displays the biggest demonstration of the oneness and equality which cannot be realized by any other means.

Thus, the institution of *Hajj* serves as the major unifying influence in Islam and the most effective common bond among the diverse believers assembling from all parts of the world. The great socializing impact of the *Hajj* has been described by P.K. Hitti in the following words:

"It afforded opportunity for Negroes, Berbers, Chinese, Persians, Syrians, Turks, Arabs-rich and poor, high and low to fraternize and meet together on the common ground of faith. Of all world religions Islam seems to have attained the largest measure of success in demolishing the barriers of race, colour and nationality."[11]

References

1. Athar Hussain, *Prophet Muhammad and His Mission*, p. 67.
2. Khwaja Kamaluddin, *The Ideal Prophet*, p. 121.
3. Lord Headley, *A Western Awakening to Islam*, pp. 22-23.
4. The Qur'an, Surah 99. Translation quoted from *The Meaning of the Glorious Koran* by M.M. Pickthall.
5. The Qur'an, Surah 101.
6. The Qur'an (CVII: 4-7).
7. The Qur'an (II: 177).
8. Quoted by Athar Husain in his book *Prophet Muhammad and His Mission*, pp. 84-85.
9. M.M. Pickthall, *The Meaning of the Glorious Koran*, p. 49.
10. *Ibid.*, p. 70.
11. P.K. Hitti, *History of the Arabs*, p. 136.

3

TOLERANCE IN ISLAM

Perhaps the ugliest aspect of human life is the fact that a great deal of blood continues to be shed by mankind in the name of religion. This is in spite of the fact that enough of human blood had already been shed in the past by members of different religious communities during the days of their political domination in the Early and Middle Ages. The irony is that Allah and His angels, to propitiate whom such acts of violence are perpetrated, only frown upon their religious stalwarts, while the Devil and his accomplices laugh heartily at the most inhuman act of human beings.

The severe persecution of the Jews by their adversaries in pre-Islamic days for the purpose of converting them to their faith by force, is too well known to need any elaboration. This is an established fact that the Jews have suffered enormously ever since they were evicted from Judea in 135 A.D. by the Romans. They were severely persecuted and a number of anti-Jewish measures were taken by their oppressors. Their position further deteriorated following the conversion of the Teutonic Barbarians from Arianism to orthodox Christianity towards the end of the sixth century A.D.[1], who ruled over the Iberian Peninsula for about two and a half centuries (456-711 A.D.)[2]. The Jews, who were the most numerous in Spain in those days, were subjected to bitter persecution by the Visigoths. Under King Sisebut (A.D. 612-21) a royal decree was issued enjoining all Jews to be baptized under penalty of banishment and confiscation of property.[3]

It is related that under the influence of terror more than ninety thousand Jews were baptized.[4] King Chintila (A.D. 636-40) forbade unconverted Jews to remain in the kingdom. King Receswinth (A.D. 649-72) prohibited the practice of the Jewish religion under pain of death.[5] Similarly, King Egica (A.D. 687-702), with a view to reducing their economic power, increased the special taxes payable by the Jews and forbade them to transact commercial business or to engage in foreign trade.[6]

Lastly, the Jews were also made the scapegoat for all sorts of corruption and disorder prevalent in the world. Michelet has described this in the following words:

> "Whenever, during the Middle Ages, men began to ask how it was that the ideal Paradise of a world under the sway of the Church was realised here below as a Hell, the Church, conscious of the objection, hastened to stifle it by declaring: It is the wrath of God. It is due to the crime of the Jews. The murderers of our Lord are still unpunished. And a persecution of the Jews was set on foot."[7]

Besides, the severe methods adopted by King Olaf Trygvesson in the propagation of Christianity in Viken (the southern part of Norway) are too well known to need repetition. He forced Christianity on the non-Christian subjects under penalty of death or banishment.[8] While the knights of "Ordo fratrum militiae Christi" succeeded in baptizing the people of Livonia by force, King Cnut forcibly rooted out paganism from his dominions in Denmark.[9]

Here, it should be clearly borne in mind that although many other instances can be mentioned where violent means were adopted by Christian propagandists for the spread of their faith, it is not intended here to attribute the expansion of Christianity exclusively to the sword by belittling the fruitful labours of peaceful Christian missionaries and saints in this regard.

Likewise, it is curious to note in this context that the Jews were not the first victims of such inhuman atrocities as were perpetrated against them by their oppressors. But when in power, they themselves had committed similar atrocities against non-Jewish population of their kingdom. While dealing with the maltreatment meted out to the Jews by the Christians in the Visigothic Kingdom, A.J. Toynbee rightly says:

> "Though the vice of fanaticism acquired the new name of bigotry from the conspicuousness of the Visigoths' practice of it, these Teutonic barbarians were not in fact the first bigots known to history. The abuse of political power for the inhuman purpose of imposing on a subject minority a choice between the abandonment of its ancestral religion and the extreme penalty of banishment or even death had been practised by the Jews against their Gentile neighbours in Syria seven hundred years before they themselves had been confronted with the same choice by the Visigoths in the Iberian Peninsula. The earliest known instance of bigotry is the compulsory conversion of the conquered Gentiles of Galilee (in north Palestine) to Judaism by their Maccabaean Jewish conqueror Alexander Jannaeus in the first quarter of the last century B.C. "[10]

Another instance of persecution by the Jews may be found in the ruthless massacre of the Christians of Najran by the Jewish King Dhu Nuwas, a fanatical adherent of Judaism, in 523 A.D. It is related that when the Christians of Najran refused to oblige the king by professing Judaism, a large number of them were killed by the sword,[11] while the remaining about twenty thousand of them[12] were thrown into a ditch which the king had got dug and filled with blazing fire.[13] About a hundred years later, while consoling and encouraging the followers of Prophet Muhammad who were then being severely persecuted by the Meccan disbelievers, the Quran referred to this ghastly tragedy in the following verses:[14]

> "Self-destroyed were the owners of the ditch
>
> Of the fuel-fed fire,
>
> When they sat by it,
>
> And were themselves the witnesses of what they did to the believers.
>
> They had naught against them save that they believed in Allah, the Mighty, the Owner of Praise."[15]

Islamic Tolerance

By drawing attention to the persecution practised by the Jews and the Christians against each other, the present writer does not seek to maintain that the Muslims were a non-violent lot. They, too, have shed human blood in abundance but with the marked difference that in their case it was mostly for political purposes. For instance, when the Abbasids seized power from their Umayyad brethren in A.D. 750, they inaugurated their triumph by slaughtering the latter indiscriminately. As described by R.A. Nicholson, "All the Ummayads were remorselessly hunted down and massacred in cold blood-even those who surrendered only on the strength of the most solemn pledges that they had nothing to fear."[16]

Further, the quantity of blood shed by the Muslims over the issue of the caliphate is too big to be exaggerated. In the words of al-Shahrastani: "Never was there an Islamic issue which brought about more bloodshed than the caliphate."[17]

These and other similar incidents will, no doubt, remain as ugly blots on the history of the Muslims. Besides, they also fought battles for the extension of their dominion over the lands of the unbelievers. But what distinguishes them from the other religious communities is the fact that they did not resort to persecution of non-Muslims for the inhuman purpose of imposing their faith on them. They seem to have gone to the utmost limits of tolerance in their treatment of the subject peoples. A brief introduction of Islamic tolerance is given below for acquaintance with the true humanitarian spirit of Islam.

Non-Muslims treated as Protected Subjects

One of the basic elements of Islamic civilization during the Middle Ages was its liberal and tolerant attitude towards members of other religions. The subject peoples were treated as *ahl al-dhimmah* (i.e., the protected people). They enjoyed freedom of faith and protection of the Muslims in return for the payment of a very moderate tax called *jizyah* (poll-tax). At first this applied only to people of the revealed religions, i.e. the Jews, Christians and Sabeans, but was later extended to include the fireworshipping Zoroastrians, the heathens of Harran, pagan Berbers of North Africa and followers of other creeds.[18] Hindus also were included among the *dhimmis*. It is related that when on the conquest of Sind by Muhammad bin al-Qasim in A.D. 711-12, a group of Brahmans approached him for the protection of their lives and temples, he granted them the status of the *dhimmis* by declaring:

"ماالبدا إلاككنائس النصارى واليهود وبيوت نيران المجوس

(The Hindu temples are just like the Christian churches, Jewish synagogues and the Zoroastrian fire-temples.)[19]

Thus, as described by Sayyid Sulayman Nadwi, the Hindus were treated by the Muslims as *ahl al-Kitab* (people of the Scripture).[20]

The Poll-Tax

Even in levying the poll-tax the Muslims fully exhibited their humane and tolerant attitude towards the non-Muslims in view of the fact that it was payable only by such of them as were capable of military service at the moderate rate of one to four dinars per year according to the size of their income, and that it was not levied upon females, children, monks, the old, the crippled, the blind and also not on paupers and slaves. In return, the Muslim state assumed full responsibility for the protection of their lives and property, and also gave them full religious and cultural freedom. They were excused from military service, and were exempt from the poor-tax payable by the Muslims for community charity.[21]

As stated above *jizyah* was imposed on the non-Muslims in return for the protection granted to them by the Muslims and also in lieu of the military service which is obligatory upon the able-bodied Muslim males. In no case this should be considered as a humiliation-tax or as a penalty for their refusal to accept Islam. This is clear from the fact that in case of participation of non-Muslim communities in the Muslim state's military services, the poll-tax was fully waived, as happened under the Indian Muslim rulers, namely, Akbar, Jahangir and Shahjahan.[22] It was also waived in cases where they could not be protected by the Muslims. It is a well-known fact that when Abu 'Ubaydah, the governor-general of Syria, found himself unable to ensure the protection of the *dhimmis* of Hims in the face of an enormous army raised by the Roman Emperor, Heraclius, to drive back the invading forces of the Muslims, he returned the amount of poll-tax collected from them, saying:

"إنما اخذنا هاجزاء منعتكم والدفاع عنكم وقدعجزنا"

(Indeed, we have collected it from you in return for protecting and defending you, but we have failed in our duty.)[23]

As a result, huge sums of money were paid back to the *dhimmis* out of the state treasury. This impressed them so much that they called down blessings of Allah on the Muslims, saying: "May God give you rule over us again and make you victorious over the Romans; had it been they, they would not have given us back anything, but would have taken all that remained with us."[24]

Moreover, the manner in which the poll-tax was collected is yet another proof of the tolerant attitude of the Muslims towards their non-Muslim subjects. The collectors of this tax were particularly instructed to show leniency and avoid all harsh treatment even in case of non-payment.[25]

Origins of Islamic Tolerance

One chief feature of Islamic tolerance is that it constitutes an essential part of the religion of Islam, as it is strictly enjoined in a number of Quranic verses and sayings of Prophet Muhammad. They not only prohibit Muslims from attempting to impose their faith on non-Muslims, but also exhort them to treat them gently and leniently. Muslim preachers are commanded to adopt only peaceful methods of preaching. They are also enjoined to practise utmost restraint, endurance and patience in their treatment of non-Muslims. Consider, for example, the following verses:

'لاإكراه فى الدين'

(There is no compulsion in religion.)[26]

'واصبرعلى مايقولون واهجرهم هجرا جميلا'

(And endure what they say with patience, and part from them with a decorous departure.)[27]

"ولاتزال تطلع على خائنة منهم الاقليلا منهم، فاعف عنهم
واصفح، ان الله يحب المحسنين'

Thou wilt not cease to discover treachery from all save a few of them. But bear with them and pardon them. Lo ! Allah loveth the kindly.)[28]

Another important aspect of the tolerant spirit of Islam is apparent in its recognition of other religions. Unlike, Judaism and Christianity, Islam recognises and respects prophets of all religions both known and unknown. No other scripture can show such texts as quoted below from the Quran:

"قل آمنا بالله وماانزل علينا وماانزل على ابراهيم واسمٰعيل واسحٰق ويعقوب والأسباط وماأوتى موسىٰ وعيسىٰ والنبيون من ربهم لا نفرق بين احدمنهم ونحن له مسلمون."

(Say, O Muhammad: We believe in Allah and that which is revealed unto us and that which was revealed unto Abraham and Ishmael and Isaac and Jacob and the tribes, and that which was vouchsafed unto Moses and Jesus and the Prophets from their Lord. We make no distinction between any of them, and unto Him we have surrendered.)[29]

"وقالوا لن يدخل الجنة الا من كان هودا اونصارى تلك امانيهم قل هاتوا برهانكم ان كنتم صادقين. بلى من اسلم وجهه لله وهو محسن فله اجره عند ربه ولا خوف عليهم ولاهم يحزنون."

(And they say: None entereth Paradise unless he be a Jew or a Christian. These are their own desires. Say: Bring your proof of what ye state if ye are truthful. Nay, but whosoever surrendereth his purpose to Allah while doing good, his reward is with his Lord; and there shall no fear come upon them neither shall they grieve.)[30]

And again:

"ان الـذيـن أمنوا والذين هادوا والنصارىٰ والصابئين من أمن بـالـلـه واليـوم الآخـروعـمـل صـالـحـا فلهم اجرهم عندربهم ولاخوف عليهم ولاهم يـحزنون"۔

(Lo! those who believe in that which is revealed unto thee, Muhammad, and those who are Jews, and Christians, and Sabaeans-whoever believeth in Allah and the Last Day and doeth right-surely their reward is with their Lord, and there shall no fear come upon them neither shall they grieve.)[31]

Besides, Muslims are bound by their religion to treat the subject peoples leniently and justly. Under no circumstances they are allowed to violate the rights granted to the *dhimmis*. Even in the case of being wronged by them they are strictly enjoined not to leave the path of justice and righteousness, as is clear from the following verse:

إنّ الـذيـن أمـنوا والذين هادوا والنصارىٰ والصابنين من آمن بـالـلـه واليـوم الآخـر وعـمـل صـالـحـا فلهم اجرهم عندربهم ولاخوف عليهم ولاهم يـحزنون۔

(O ye who believe ! Be stedfast witnesses for Allah in equity, and let not hatred of any people seduce you that ye deal not justly. Deal justly, that is nearer to your duty. Observe your duty to Allah. Lo! Allah is informed of what ye do.)[32]

Apparently, it is not possible for the Muslims to observe all these Quranic injunctions except with a very high level of tolerance, restraint and patience on their part.

Tolerance as preached and practised by Prophet Muhammad and early Caliphs

Tolerance and forgiveness were the chief ingredients of Prophet Muhammad's character. He did not lose his patience even in the most adverse conditions. In fact, his patience increased in the face of insolence and revilement. He never invoked the curse of Allah even upon his bitterest enemies. It is related that when he was wounded at Uhud, his Companions were so deeply chagrined that they said to him: "Wouldst thou not invoke the Lord's wrath against the disbelievers?" Far from obliging them, he replied: "I have not been sent to invoke evil upon man but to pray for the Lord's favour and mercy unto him".

Such unparalleled display of tolerance and magnanimity not only gives an insight into the Prophet's character, but also throws sufficient light on the true nature of Islam. He forgave even his assailants, and took pity on them. Their ignorance of his mission was to him a sufficient cause for taking pity on them. Hence, he prayed for their guidance.[33]

The Prophet's mode of dealing with non-Muslims is marked by a large-hearted tolerance and sympathy. Contrary to what has been alleged by some Western historians, he meted out a kind and gentle treatment to them not only in the early years of his prophethood, but also in the later years when he was at the height of his power and at the head of a large army.[34] For example, it is related by Abu Basrah Ghifari that, while still a non-Muslim, he once went to the Prophet and stayed with him as a guest. In the night, he drank the whole of milk yielded by the goats of his host. The Prophet did not show any resentment, although, the members of his family remained hungry that night.[35] It is curious to note that far from viewing non-Muslims with disfavour, he showed respect and courtesy to them as well as encouraged friendly and social relations between them and his followers. Numerous instances can be stated in support of this point. Here, it will suffice to mention that when the child of a certain Jew fell ill, he visited the sick child. On yet another occasion, when the funeral procession of a Jew passed by him, he stood out of respect and courtesy for it.[36] And the way, he treated the delegation of the Christians of Najran has no parallel in the history of other conquerors. He not only played host to them and lodged them in the Prophetic Mosque, but also permitted them to offer prayers on Christian lines in the same Mosque.[37]

The Prophet was so full of care for the safety and well-being of the *dhimmis* that he enjoined his followers not to harm them in any way, saying :

"من أذىٰ ذميا، فليس منا"

(Whoever harms a *dhimmi*, does not belong to us.)

This tradition has been described by the celebrated Arab historian, al-Baladhuri, in the following words: "Whoever wrongs one with whom a compact has been made, (i.e. a *dhimmi*) and lays on him a burden beyond his strength, I will be his accuser."[38]

Similarly, each of the first four rightly-guided Caliphs of Islam, namely, Abu Bakr, 'Umar bin al-Khattab, 'Uthman and 'Ali, took particular care to ensure protection of the lives, property and places of worship of the non-Muslims. An idea of the toleration extended by the early Caliphs to their non-Muslim subjects may be derived from the fact that when the Christians of Hirah capitulated to Khalid bin al-Walid, he issued a proclamation guaranteeing their lives, liberty and property, and declared that they were free to perform their religious rites and take out their crosses on occasions of festivals. As described by Imam Abu Yusuf, the Chief Judge of Harun al-Rashid, this declaration was duly approved of and sanctioned by Caliph Abu Bakr and his Consultative Council consisting of 'Umar, 'Uthman, 'Ali and other leading Companions of the Prophet.[39]

Caliph 'Umar bin al-Khattab deserves special mention in this connection. He is credited with having set a precedent by granting a number of fundamental rights to the *dhimmis*. Besides allowing them full religious freedom, he granted them the rights to equality, honour, speech and livelihood. In matters of civil and criminal judicial procedure they were allowed the jurisdiction of their own canon laws as administered by the respective heads of their religious communities. They had an equal status before law. In the administration of justice there was no difference between the rulers and the ruled. A Muslim murderer of a non-Muslim was given capital punishment.

When the Caliph visited Jerusalem on its capitulation to the Muslims in 638 A.D., he refused to offer prayers in the Church of the Holy Sepulchre, lest his followers should make that a pretext for converting it into a mosque.[40] And the following charter of security granted by the Caliph to the people of Jerusalem served as a model for future arrangements with the remaining Syro-Palestinian cities:

> "In the name of God, the Merciful, the Compassionate, this is the security which 'Umar, the servant of God, the commander of the faithful, grants to the people of Aelia. He grants to all, whether sick or sound, security for their lives, their possessions, their churches and their crosses, and for all that concerns their religion. Their churches shall not be changed into dwelling places, nor destroyed, neither shall they nor their appurtenances be in any way diminished, nor the crosses of the inhabitants nor aught of their possessions, nor shall

any constraint be put upon them in the matter of their faith, nor shall anyone of them be harmed."[41]

The liberal and secular attitude of the Caliph is also evidenced by the fact that he allowed the Jews to enter Jerusalem for the first time after they had been kept away from it by the Romans for centuries. This was the main reason why the Jews joined the Muslims in its defence when it was besieged by the Crusaders in 1099 A.D. And again a rapid growth of Palestinian Jewry followed the recapture of the city by Salah al-Din al-Ayyubi in 1167 A.D.[43]

It was in keeping with the Caliph's spirit of kindness and consideration for the *dhimmis* that he paid regular old-age pensions from the Public Treasury to such non-Muslims also as were unable to earn their livelihood. He was so seriously concerned with their well-being that even at his death-bed, he did not forget them. He is recorded to have advised his successor, Caliph 'Uthman, to look after their interests, saying:

"اوصى الخليفة من بعدى بذمة رسول الله، ان يوفى لهم بعهدهم، وان يقاتل من ورائهم ولا يكلفهم فوق طاقتهم."

(I commend to the care of the Caliph after me the protection of the Apostle of Allah (granted to the *dhimmis*); he should keep the agreement made with them, defend them against their enemies, and should not task them beyond their strength.)[44]

The General Position of *Dhimmis* in Islam

The *dhimmis* were treated as free citizens of the state and were held in all transactions of daily life on a footing of equality with the Muslims. They occupied important clerical, executive, financial and professional positions in the government. They developed wealth and learning, and were entrusted with posts of high responsibility. Almost all administrative posts of high salaries and trust were open to them equally with the Muslims. They were often appointed as rectors of Muslim universities and educational institutions as well as curators of Muslim endowments.[45] Under the Mughal Emperors of India, the Hindus not only participated in the deliberations of the councils of the sovereign, but also commanded armies and administered provinces.[46]

An idea of the trust reposed by Muslim rulers in the *dhimmis* may be derived from the fact that Hasday ben Shaprut, a renowned Jewish physician and scholar, was appointed by Caliph 'Abd al-Rahman al-Nasir (A.D. 912-61) as Chief Treasurer of the state. Under his influence a large number of Jewish scholars and men of letters settled in Muslim Spain, and Cordova became the centre of Talmudic researches and studies.[47] In fact, this marks the beginning of the flowering of Jewish culture in Muslim Spain. Besides, most of the personal physicians of Muslim rulers were non-Muslims, mainly Christians. Of them mention may be made of the Nestorian Jurjis ibn Bakhtishu', the court physician of Caliph al-Mansur. He is said to have become the founder of a family which for about seven generations, covering a period of two centuries and a half, held monopoly over the court medical practice.[48] Among numerous other non-Muslim dignitaries, some were appointed as vizirs. Caliph al-Muttaqi (A.D. 940-44) had a Christian vizir, as did one of the Buwayhids, while Caliph al-Mu'tadid (A.D. 892-902) had a Christian as head of the war office.[49]

It is, of course, true that in some cases, very few in number, discriminatory legislation was passed against the non-Muslims, mainly the Christians and Jews, obliging them to pay respect to the Muslims, to wear a distinctive dress, and to ride only on mules and asses. But this should be clearly borne in mind that the promulgation of such discriminatory laws was an exception rather than the rule in view of the fact that in the long history of Islam only four Caliphs, namely, the Umayyad 'Umar II, Harun al-Rashid, al-Mutawakkil and the

Fatimid al-Hakim, are charged with having enacted and renewed discriminatory measures against the *dhimmis*.[51] Since such discrimination had no sanction in the Quran or in the practice of the Prophet, this should not be taken as characteristic of the Muslim rule.[52] On the face of it, this may better be termed as un-Islamic. It is curious to note that even in the' few exceptional cases where such discriminatory legislation was passed, it mostly remained "ink on paper" and was never seriously implemented.[53]

That in spite of these occasional discriminatory measures the *dhimmis* enjoyed under the Muslim rule a large measure of toleration may be inferred from the high level of communal autonomy, economic prosperity and cultural flowering realized and attained by them. The Jews, as noted above, developed a vigorous economic and cultural life. They enjoyed self-government under their "exilarch" who was accepted by the caliphs as religious head of all the Jews in Iraq, Armenia, Turkistan, Persia and Yemen. Their rabbinical academies at Sura and Pumbeditha provided religious and intellectual leadership to the Jews of *dar al-Islam*.[54] Their religious leader lived in affluence. He wore a diadem on his turban, and appeared dressed in embroidered silk. Whenever, he rode through the city of Baghdad, which was the centre of Eastern Hebrews, he was honoured by the Muslims as well, while men heralded ahead of him calling out: "Make way for our Lord, the Son of David."[55] A tax was also levied by him on markets, merchandise and inns. And in the words of C.R. Conder, "The Baghdad synagogue had pillars of coloured marble plated with silver and gold, and the city seems to have been the Paradise of Israel during an age of persecution in Europe."[56]

Likewise, the Nestorian patriarch or catholicos exercised a certain measure of jurisdiction over the Christians in the Muslim empire. The patriarch was recognised by the Caliphs as the official head of the Christians. That they freely carried on their missionary work is evidenced by the fact that their missionaries went as far as India and China under the protection of the Muslims.[57]

Lastly, some of the best evidences of the toleration of the Muslim government in general are furnished by the non-Muslims themselves. A few of them may appropriately be mentioned here. In the reign of Caliph 'Uthman, the Christian Patriarch of Merv spoke to the Bishop of Fars, named Simeon, of the liberal and generous attitude of the Arabs towards their Christian friends in the following words:

> "The Arabs who have been given by God the kingdom (of the earth) do not attack the Christian faith; on the contrary they help us in our religion; they respect our God and our Saints, and bestow gifts on our churches and monasteries."[58]

Similarly, while commenting on the position of the Christians in Muslim Spain, Reinhart Dozy, the author of *Spanish Islam*, says:

> "The condition of the Christians under the Moslems, compared with what it had been formerly, was therefore not one of great hardship. The unbounded tolerance of the Arabs must also be taken into account. In religious matters, they put pressure on no man. The Christians were not ungrateful. They were under obligations to their conquerors for the tolerance and justice shown them; and preferred their rule to that of, for instance, the Franks."[59]

And again, Israel Zangwill, a noted Jewish scholar, has described the political status of the Jews under the Muslim rule by comparing the tolerant Arabs with the Christians in the following words:

> "Under the new Arab regime all Jewish disabilities were swept away, and the sole tribute imposed was of one golden dinar per head. Even apart from the

> new political status, life must have grown easier amid fellow-monotheists and fellow-Semites, whose very language approximated to the idiom of the synagogue. The Christians who had oppressed them were a rude, ignorant rabble, compared with the courtly, learned and luxurious Moors, whose advance over Europe represented a real wave of *Kulture* (culture)."[60]

In short, tolerance was a firmly established principle of Muslim policy dating from the time of Prophet Muhammad himself. In the words of Goldziher," Islam pushed this policy to extreme limits. In India, for example, the old rites were celebrated in the temples under Muslim rule."[61]

It is in view of these facts that the virtuous quality of Islamic tolerance has been described by M.M. Pickthall as given below:

> "In order that the world may see it (Islam) as it is, we must set forth this great virtue of Islamic tolerance—a tolerance which the rest of the world did not begin even to contemplate till many centuries later, a tolerance which even the West, with all its progress, has not yet attained."[62]

Thus, the freedom of faith and opinion, a pre-requisite for scientific investigation, was the most sophisticated tool of civilization wielded by the Muslims, during the Middle Ages. In fact, it was this freedom, together with Islamic tolerance, munificent patronage of learning and protection of the minorities, which not only made possible the rich cultural heritage of the Muslims, but also was responsible for the economic prosperity and educational and cultural flowering of the subject peoples, mainly the Jews, Christians and Indians—the peoples who have lived in close contacts with the Muslims under the latter's protection for long periods of time.

References

1. Will Durant: *The Story of Civilization*, Vol. IV, p. 95.
2. *Ibid.*, p. 95.
3. A.J. Toynbee: *A Study of History*, Vol. VIII, p. 279.
4. R. Dozy: *Spanish Islam*, tr. by F.G. Stokes, p. 227.
5. A.J. Toynbee, *op.cit.*, p. 278.
6. *Ibid.*, 279.
7. R. Dozy, *op.cit.*, p. 227.
8. T.W. Arnold, *The Preaching of Islam*, p. 8.
9. *Ibid.*, p. 7.
10. A.J. Toynbee, *op.cit.*, p. 279.
11. R.A. Nicholson: *A Literary History of the Arabs*, p. 26.
12. R. Dozy, *op.cit.*, p. 15.
13. R.A. Nicholson, *op.cit.*, p. 26.
14. The Qur'an: 85(4-8).
15. M.M. Pickthall: *The Meaning of the Glorious Koran*, p. 435.
16. R.A. Nicholson, *op.cit.*, p. 253.
17. P.K. Hitti, *History of the Arabs*, p. 139.
18. *Ibid.*, p. 233.
19. Al-Baladhuri, *Futuh-ul-Buldan*, p. 439.
20. Sayyid Sulayman Nadwi, *Arab wa Hind ke Ta'alluqat*, p. 194.
21. Will Durant, *op.cit.*, p. 218.
22. Aziz Ahmad, *Studies in Islamic Culture in the Indian Environment*, pp. 80-81.

23. Dr. Husain Fawzi al-Najjar, *"Al-'Uhud w-al-Mawathiqf-il-Islam"*, published in the journal *Al-Arabi*, Kuwait, No. 204,1975, p. 27.

24. T.W. Arnold, *op.cit.*, p. 61.

25. *Ibid.*, p. 60.

26. The Qur'an: (11: 256).

27. The Qur'an: (LXXIII: 10).

28. The Qur'an: (V: 13).

29. The Qur'an: (III: 84) tr. by M.M. Pickthall.

30. The Qur'an: (II: 111-12), tr. by M.M. Pickthal.

31. The Qur'an: (II: 62), tr. by M.M. Pickthall.

32. The Qur'an: (V: 8), tr. by M.M. Pickthall.

33. Prof. Sheikh Youssef El-Digway: *Messages of Peace*, p. 131.

34. Shibli Nu'mani: *Sirat-ul-Nabi*, Vol. I, p. 292.

35. *Ibid.*, p. 292.

36. *Ibid.*, p. 296.

37. *Ibid.*, p. 296.

38. T.W. Arnold, *op.cit.*, p. 77.

39. Sayed Ameer Ali: *The Spirit of Islam*, p. 272.

40. T.W. Arnold, *op.cit.*, p. 57.

41. *Ibid.*, p. 56.

42. *"Al-Izdihar-ul-Yahudi fi zill-il-Imbraturiyat-il-Islamiyah"* by Ahmad Baha'uddin, published in the Journal *Al-Arabi*, Kuwait, No. 252, p. 17.

43. Will Durant, *op.cit.*, p. 366.

44. Dr. Husain Fawzi al-Najjar, *op.cit.*, p. 26.

45. Syed Ameer Ali, *op.cit.*, p. 275.
46. *Ibid.*, p. 276.
47. Ahmad Baha'uddin, *op.cit.*, p. 12.
48. P.K. Hitti, *op.cit.*, p. 309.
49. *Ibid.*, p. 355.
50. *Ibid.*, p. 353.
51. *Ibid.*, pp. 333-54.
52. Aziz Ahmad, *op.cit.*, p. 90,
53. P.K. Hitti, *op.cit.*, p. 353.
54. Will Durant, *op.cit.*, p. 366.
55. C.R. Conder: *The Latin Kingdom of Jerusalem*, p. 244.
56. *Ibid.*, p. 245.
57. P.K. Hitti, *op.cit.*, pp. 355-56.
58. Syed Ameer Ali, *op.cit.*, p. 274.
59. R. Dozy, *op.cit.*, p. 235.
60. Speeches, Articles and Letters of Israel Zangwill, ed. by Maurice Simon, p. 115.
61. Goldziher, *Die Religion des Islams*, p. 106.
62. M.M. Pickthall, "Muslim Education" in *Golden Jubilee Commoemoration Volume of the Islamic Culture (1927-76)*, Hyderabad, p. 21.

4

The Status of Women in Islam

In the pre-Islamic times women occupied a very low position in the social scale. They were treated like a mere chattel marketable and transferable. They neither enjoyed any freedom, nor had any right. Their condition remained miserable in all parts of the world.

In ancient Greece, women were not allowed to join men in social gatherings. They never joined the study circles of philosophers. Harlots, divorced women and courtesan slave-girls enjoyed a greater title to fame and respect than married women. Even Plato, the great lover of wisdom used to say : "I thank God that I was born Greek and not barbarian, freeman and not slave, man and not women."[1]

Likewise, Aristotle expressed his contempt for women by censuring Spartans for being kind to their womenfolk and giving them the rights of inheritance, divorce and self-dependence, and considered these as the reasons for the downfall of Sparta.

In ancient India, the woman's position was equally deplorable. She could never dream of becoming self-dependent. The laws of Manu accorded her no individuality save that as dependent on her father or husband. She could neither inherit nor possess property, and after her husband's death, she became a client of their eldest son. Her husband could even chastise her with the bamboo-rod.[2] Remarriage of the widows was quite out of question. They were 'treated as the most unfortunate creatures on earth. That was the main reason why they were required to die on the funeral pyres of their dead husbands. It was an age-old custom followed from the ancient days of Brahmanic civilization. It was only in the seventeenth century that this horrible custom was given up owing to rising public opinion against it.

Judaism and Christianity did little to ameliorate the lot of women. An idea of the Jewish attitude towards the fair sex may be derived from the fact that Orthodox Jews still have in their official prayer book the following :

> "Blessed art thou, our Lord, our God, who has not made me a woman". Also Jehova said to the woman: "I shall greatly increase the pain of your pregnancy; in pangs you will bring forth children, and your craving will be for, your husband, and he will dominate you."[3]

Similarly, the Church of Christ had placed the sex under a ban. Their priests had written upon the enormities of women, their evil tendencies, their inconceivable malignity. Tertullian represented the general feeling in a book, in which he described women as the devil's gateway, the unsealer of the forbidden tree, the deserter of the divine law, the destroyer of God's men.[4] As described by Lecky, Chrysostom, a saint of high merit, "interpreted the general opinion of the Fathers when he, pronounced women to be a necessary evil, a natural temptation, a desirable calamity, a domestic peril, a deadly fascination, a painted ill."[5] The orthodox Chruch excluded women from the exercise of all religious functions. They were excluded absolutely from society. They were prohibited from appearing in public, from going to feasts or banquets. They were directed to remain in seclusion, to observe silence, to obey their husbands, and to apply themselves to weaving and spinning and cooking.[6] In short, the woman was condemned as the most potent source of sin and temptation. According to the creation story of the *Genesis*, it was Eve who tempted Adam to eat the forbidden fruit, and thus laid the burden of original sin upon man. In view of this belief some orthodox monasteries in Greece prohibited not only women but also female domestic animals from entering their premises.[7] Such was the position of women in Christianity.

The condition of women among the pre-Islamic Arabs was also degraded in the extreme. They had no social status. Like their counterparts elsewhere, they were kept deprived of the right of inheritance. They were inherited by the heirs of their deceased husbands like their property. The pagan Arabs held women in utmost contempt, ill-treated and hated them habitually. They considered the birth of a daughter as a calamity, and buried alive many of their female children. Their shameful attitude towards women is summed up in the following Verse of the Quran:

" واذا بشر احدهم بالاُنثى ظلّ وجهه مسودا وهو كظيم۔
يتوارى من القوم من سوء ما بشربه، ايمسكه على هون ام
يدسه فى التراب، الاساء مايحكمون۔" (XVI : 58-59)

(When if one of them receiveth tidings of the birth of a female, his face remaineth darkened, and he is wroth inwardly. He hideth himself from the folk because of the evil of that whereof he hath had tidings, (asking himself): Shall he keep it in contempt, or bury it beneath the dust. Verily evil is their judgement.)[8]

Respect for Women in Islam

When Islam came, far-reaching reforms were introduced for raising the social end economic conditions of women. It not only paid attention to their uplift in society, but also restored to them all their genuine and natural rights as well as put them on a footing of equality with men by commanding its followers to treat them with respect and kindness. The Quran has forbidden the pre-Islamic injustices to women in the following words:

"يٰأيها الذين آمنوا لا يحلّ لكم ان ترثوا النساء كرهاء ولاتعضلوهن لتذهبوا ببعض ماآتيتموهن إلّا ان ياتين بفاحشة مبينة وعاشروهن بالمعروف فان كرهتموهن فعسى ان تكرهوا شيئا ويجعل الله فيه خيرا كثيرا." (IV:19)

> (O ye who believe ! It is not lawful for you forcibly to inherit the women (of your deceased kinsmen), nor that ye should put constraint upon them that ye may take away a part of that which ye have given them, unless they be guilty of flagrant lewdness. But consort with them in kindness, for if ye hate it may happen that ye hate a-thing wherein Allah hath placed much good.)[9]

It goes to the credit of Islam that it enjoined respect for women as daughters, sisters, wives and mothers at a time when their counterparts of the world suffered humiliation and were looked down upon in all spheres of life. The position of wife and mother is highly exalted in Islamic tradition. Prophet Muhammad is reported to have said: "The best among you is the one who is best towards his wife." His last sermon delivered at Mecca contained these memorable words: "Treat your wives well; they are your helpers and can do nothing by themselves". Raising the position of women, the Prophet has gone so far as to say: "Even Paradise lies underneath the feet of your mothers."

As reported by al-Bukhari, someone once asked the Prophet which work pleased Allah most. His reply was: "Worship at the appointed hour". And to the question: "And what afterwards?", the Prophet's reply was: "To be bounteous to your father and mother". Thus, he deserves the greatest gratitude of humanity for the revolutionary steps taken by him in raising the status of women to the greatest possible extent. It should be no exaggeration to say that had he done nothing more, his claim to be a benefactor of humanity would have been indisputable.

Equal Status of Men and Women

The attitude adopted by Islam about the equality of men and women is quite in line with human nature. The Quran attributes the existence of mankind to partnership of men and women. It does not discriminate between them on the basis of sex. Both are promised the same reward for good deeds, the same punishment for evil conduct. The status granted to women by Islam is adequately expressed in the following Verses:

"من عمل صالحا من ذكر اوانثى وهومؤمن فلنحيينه حيواة
طيبة ولنجزينهم اجرهم باحسن ما كانوا يعملون."

(XVI : 97)

(Whosoever doeth right, whether male or female, and is a believer, him verily We shall quicken with good life, and We shall pay them a recompense in proportion to the best of what they used to do.)[10]

"ان المسلمين والمسلمات والمؤمنين والمؤ منات والقانتين والقانتات والصٰدقين والصٰدقات والصابرين والصابرات والخٰشعين والخٰشعٰت والمتصدقين والمتصدقات والصائمين و الصائمات والحٰفظين فروجهم والحٰفظٰت والذاكراين الله كثيراوالذاكرات، اعدّاللّه لهم مغفرة واجراًعظيما۔"

(XXXIII :35)

(Lo! men who surrender unto Allah, and women who surrender, and men who believe and women who believe, and men who obey and women who obey, and men who speak the truth and women who speak the truth, and men who persevere in righteousness and women who persevere, and men who are humble and women who are humble, and men who give alms and women who give alms, and men who fast and women who fast, and men who guard their modesty and women who guard their modesty, and men who remember Allah much and women who remember-Allah prepared for them forgiveness and a vast reward.)[11]

" فاستجاب لهم ربهم انى لااضيع عمل عامل منكم من ذكر او انثى، بعضكم من بعض......" (195: III)

(And their Lord hath heard them (and He saith) : Lo! I suffer not the work of any worker, male or female, to be lost. Ye proceed one from another.)[12]

The expression-"ye proceed one from another"-recurs in the Quran. It is a reminder to men that women are of the same human status as themselves. These and like passages in the Quran are sufficient to show that utterly mistaken are those who make reckless and false statements regarding the position of women in Islam.

Islam has made it clear that both men and women have special gifts from Allah. None of them is inferior or superior to the other. Both are equally important in their respective spheres of activity. While granting similar rights and rewards to both men and women, Islam does recognise the physical difference in the constitution of both of them. As such it does not wish or encourage women to assimilate themselves to men. The following observation made by Dr. Harry Campbell on the inherent nature of men and women fully justifies the Islamic concept of equality of women with men :

> "Women have smaller lungs and fewer blood cells then men. In women the vital fire does not burn so quickly. It is thus obvious that women are not adapted like men for a strenuous muscular life. Mentally men and women differ in the realm of feeling rather than of intellect. Intellectually men and women stand somewhat upon the same footing. While genius is more common in the male sex, so also is idiocy."[13]

Rights Granted to Women

While women of the West had to struggle for so many centuries to obtain recognition of their legal end civil existence, their counterparts in Islam enjoyed an independent and honourable status in society as equal partners of men. In order to inspire self-reliance, self-respect and courage among women, several civil, legal and economic rights were granted to women by Islam.

Islam stressed the importance of knowledge as an essential and unavoidable need for both men and women to achieve perfection in life. Inspired by the teachings of Islam, numerous Muslim women achieved eminence as teachers, guides, educationists, litterateurs, memorisers of the Quran and narrators of Traditions. They are held in high esteem by the Muslims even today. For example, Zubaidah, the wife of Caliph Harun, was a highly educated and cultured lady of her age, who, by her virtues and accomplishments, has left an honoured name to posterity. Humaidah, the wife of Faruq, a Medinite citizen, was the sole guardian of her minor son Rabya ar-Ray in the absence of her husband, and educated him to become one of the most distinguished jurisconsults of the day. Sukainah, the daughter of Husain, was the most brilliant and the most accomplished women of her time. The ladies of the Prophet's family were also noted for learning, their virtues, and their strength of character. Buran, the wife of Caliph Mamun; Umm-ul-Fazl, Mamun's sister; and Umm-ul-Habib, Mamun's daughter, were all famous for their scholarship.[14]

Another important priviledge of the Muslim woman is that she has the right to ratify or annual her marriage. Marriage, according to Islam, is a bilateral contract based on the free consent of the two contracting parties. It is true that the parents assist by their counsel and experience in the selection of a suitable marriage partner for their child, but it is the couple who has the last say in this matter. In this respect there is no difference between man and women in the eyes of the law. There are clear Quranic injunctions prohibiting men from infringing the women's right in this regard as mentioned below:

"واذاطلقتم النساء فبلغن اجلهن فلاتعضلوهن ان ينكحن

ازواجهن اذاتراضعوا بينهم بالمعروف ذلك يوعظ به من كان

منكم يؤ من بالله واليوم الأخر......" (II : 232)

(And when ye have divorced women and they reach their term, place not difficulties in the way of their marrying their husbands if it is agreed between them in kindness. This is an admonition for him among you who believeth in Allah and the Last Day...)[15]

"والـذيـن يتـوفـون مـنـكم ويذرون ازواجايتربصن بانفسهن
اربعة اشهر وعشرا فاذابلغن اجلهنّ فلاجناح عليكم فيما فعلن
فى انفسهن بالمعروف، والله بما تعملون خبير." (II : 234)

(Such of you as die and leave behind them wives, they (the wives) shall wait, keeping themselves apart, four months and ten days. And when they reach the term (prescribed for them) then there is no sin for you in aught that they may do with themselves in decency. Allah is informed of what ye do.)[16]

The Prophet also ordained that the woman's consent must be obtained before she is married to anyone. The widow is required to declare her consent openly, while in the case of a virgin girl her silence or tacit consent is interpreted as her acceptance of the marriage proposal. Under no circumstances she can be married without her consent.

It is of paramount importance to note that the Muslim woman retains her individuality even after her marriage. She has the right to enter into contracts and other transactions such as the buying, selling and mortgaging of goods, etc. She is free to own property and dispose of it according to her will without reference to her father or husband. This was not obtained by women in the West until the end of the nineteenth century when the Married Women's Property Acts finally abolished the rule in England where a woman's property passed to her husband after marriage. By contrast, Islam has always allowed a married woman to run a business of her own without consulting her husband and with no obligation to contribute to the 'household expenses'[17] She can even appoint an attorney to act on her behalf in legal proceedings. She is also entitled to a share in the property left by her parents and near relations. This is described in the Quran as follows:

"للرجال نصيب مما ترك الوالدان والأقربون، وللنساء نصيب مما ترك الوالدان والأقربون مما قلّ منه اوكثر، نصيبا مفروضا." (IV : 7)

> (Unto the men (of a family) belongeth a share of that which parents and near kindred leave, and unto the women a share of that which parents and near kindred leave whether it be little or much-a legal share.)[18]

As regards the quantity of inheritance, the Quran says : "To the male the equivalent of the portion of two females".[19] Some critics of Islam argue on the basis of this Verse that the Islamic law of inheritance treats women as inferior to men, for the former are given only half of the share allotted to the latter. But such criticism is not justified in view of the responsibility and function of the woman in family. It is man alone who is burdened with the responsibility of shouldering all the financial obligations of his family. He is required to provide the sustenance of his wife, children and poor relatives as well as to pay the woman's dowry as an expression of his desire to marry her. But the woman is under no such obligation. Thus the woman's share in an inheritance as allotted by Islam is quite justified.

Besides, both men and women are equal before the law. They are subject to the same punishments, or rewards in similar cases. Compensation for killing a woman is the same as in case of intentional killing of a man. The Quranic Verses dealing with compensation for killing are the same in respect of both men and women:

" ومـاكـان لمؤ من ان يقتل مؤمنا الا خطأ ومن قتل مؤمنا خطأ فتحريررقبة مؤمنة ودية مسلمة الى اهله الا ان يصدقوا......"

(IV : 92)

(It is not for a believer to kill a believer unless it be by mistake. He who hath killed a believer by mistake must set free a believing slave, and pay the blood-money to the family of the slain, unless they remit it as a charity.)[20]

" ومن يقتل مؤمنا متعمداً فجزاء ه جهنم خلدا فيها وغضب الله عليه ولعنه واعدّ له عذابا عظيما۔" (IV : 93)

(Whoso slayeth a believer of set purpose, his reward is Hell for ever. Allah is wroth against him and He hath cursed him and prepared for him an awful doom.)[21]

Another great benefit done to women by Islam is that it has put an end to the old contempt for widows by sanctioning their marriage. It has also legalised divorce, thus transforming marriage from a stage of bondage for the woman to a civil contract between equals, terminable by the will of either party.

Divorced becomes a necessity when husband and wife are in a state of perpetual conflict. This is natural that the dissatisfied couple should be freed from the marriage tie for the welfare of the household, children and society.

While legalising divorce utmost care has been taken to discourage this practice. A chance is also given to the couple for reconciliation within a prescribed period. This is clear from the following Verse :

"...... و بعولتهن احق بردهن فی ذلك ان ارادوا اصلا حا......"

(II : 228)

(... And their husbands would do better to take them back in that case if they desire a reconciliation...)[22]

The improvement effected in the position of women by Islam has been acknowledged by several unprejudiced writers. The views expressed by two Western scholars on this subject are given below:

N.J. Coulson:

"Without doubt it is the general subject of the position of women, married women in particular, which occupies the place of pride in the Quranic laws. Rules on marriage and divorce are numerous and varied, and with their general objective of improvement of women's status, represent some of the most radical reforms of the Arabian customary law effected in the Quran. She is now endowed with a legal competence she did not possess before. In the laws of divorce the supreme innovation of the Quran lies in the introduction of the 'waiting period' *(idda)*".[23]

A. Dorner:

"Certainly the Prophet raised the status of women above that assigned to them in ancient Arabia; in particular the woman was no longer a mere heritable chattel of her deceased husband's estate, but was herself capable of inheriting; while again, a free woman could not now be forced into marriage, and, in cases of divorce the husband was required to let the wife retain what he gave her at marriage. Moreover, women of the upper classes might occupy themselves with poetry and science, and even act as teachers, while those of lower rank not seldom shared the joys and sorrows of their husbands as mistresses of their households. The mother likewise must be treated with respect."[24]

References

1. W. Durant: *The Story of Philosophy*, 1960, p. 12.
2. *Encyclopaedia of Religion and Ethics*, Vol. V, p. 271.
3. Quoted by Moh. Wassel in his article "The Dynamic Equilibrium in Marriage and Divorce in Islam" in *Hamdard Islamicus*, Pakistan, Vol. VII, No. 3, p. 40.
4. Ameer Ali, *The Spirit of Islam*, p. 251.
5. *Ibid.*, p. 252.
6. *Ibid.*, p. 252.
7. Maryam Jameelah. *Islam Versus Ahl al-Kitab, Past and Present*, p. 298.
8. M.M. Pickthall: *The Meaning of the Glorious Koran*, pp. 198-99.
9. *Ibid.*, p. 81.
10. *Ibid.*, p. 201.
11. *Ibid.*, p. 304.
12. *Ibid.*, p. 78.
13. M.M. Pickthall, *Cultural Side of Islam*, p. 146.
14. Syed Ameer Ali, *The Spirit of Islam*, pp. 254-55.

15. M.M. Pickthall, *The Meaning of the Glorious Koran*, p. 54.
16. *Ibid.*, p. 54.
17. *Hamdard Islamicus*, Pakistan, Vol. VII, No. 3, p. 49.
18. M.M. Pickthall, *op.cit.*, p. 80.
19. The Quran : (IV : 11).
20. M.M. Pickthall, *op.cit.*, p. 88.
21. *Ibid.*, p. 88.
22. *Ibid.*, p. 53.
23. N.J. Coulson, *Islamic Surveys : A History of Islamic Law*, 1971, p. 14.
24. *Encyclopaedia of Religion and Ethics*, Vol. V, 1960, p. 271.

5

Humanistic Aspects of Conditional Polygamy in Islam

A large number of books have been written by European Orientalists and sociologists in condemnation of the institution of polygamy in Islam. It is described by them as one of the chief offences of this religion against the fair sex. They tend to look upon it as a religiously sanctioned prerogative of the 'superior man' to enjoy himself sexually by marrying upto four of the 'inferior woman'. They also regard Islam as a religion of sensuality. They seek to support their argument by saying that Prophet Muhammad permitted four wives, and he himself had a great many wives. Thus, they find fault with Islam only because it does not enjoin strict monogamy.

Embarrassed by this and similar propagated misrepresentation of Islamic polygamy, some Muslim writers have started holding the view that polygamy was retained by Islam only as a temporary measure to meet the needs of Muslim society during the early years of nascent Islam, and that it was no longer relevant and applicable in modern times. They support their viewpoint by quoting the Qur'anic Verses dealing with this subject out of context. They argue that if a person is not capable of dealing equitably between his wives, he should remain content with only one marriage as directed in the following Verse:

"وان خفتم الا تقسطوا فی الیتمی فانکحوا ماطاب لکم من
النساء مثنیٰ وثلث وربع، فان خفتم الا تعدلوا فواحده اوملکت
ایمانکم ذلك ادنیٰ الا تعولوا۔" (IV:3)

> (And if ye fear that ye will not deal fairly by the orphans, marry of the women, who seem good to you, two or three or four; and if ye fear that ye cannot do justice to so many then one only or the captives that your right hands possess. Thus, it is more likely that ye will not do injustice.)[1]

The critics further maintain that it is not possible for man to do full justice to all his wives despite his best efforts to do so. In support of this point the following line from the Qur'an is quoted by them out of the context :

ولن تستطیعوا ان تعدلوا بین النساء ولوحرصتم
(IV:129)......

> (Ye will not be able to deal equitably between your wives, however much ye wish to do so.)[2]

On the basis of the above Verses it is concluded by them that polygamy is prohibited in Islam. Consider, for exemple, the following statement by Syed Ameer Ali:

> "*Adl* (equity) signifies not merely equality of treatment in the matter of lodgment, clothing and other domestic requisites, but also complete equity in love, affection and esteem. As absolute justice in

matters of feeling is impossible, the Koranic prescription amounted in reality to a prohibition".[3]

But a perusal of the full text of the above Verse in the context of its subsequent lines as quoted below clearly reveals that man is permitted to marry upto four wives on condition that he deals as equitably between them as humanly possible, even though he may not be able to do full justice to all of them in matters of feeling in the strictest possible sense:

"ولن تستطيعوا ان تعدلوا بين النساء ولوحرصتم، فلاتميلوا كل الميل فتذروها كالمعلقة وان تصلحوا وتتقوا، فان الله كان غفوراً رحيماً" (IV:129)

(Ye will not be able to deal equitably between your wives, however much ye wish to do so. But turn not altogether away from one, leaving her as in suspense. if ye do good and keep from evil, lo! Allah is Forgiving, Merciful.)[4]

It is clear from the above Verses that both the Western critics as well as Muslim modernists advocating for the abolition of poligamy are quite ignorant of the true nature and significance of the conditional and modified form of polygamy as retained by Islam, the relevance or otherwise of which can be better appreciated only in the context of its historical background.

Historical Background of Polygamy

Islam is so much criticised on account of its conditional sanction of polygamy that casual readers are misled into considering it as the very originator of this institution. But this is far from being the case. The history of polygamy goes back to the ancient times. It seems to have been common in high stara of the population in ancient Hindu society. Its practice among the Vedic Indians is abundantly proved by direct references in the Rigveda and other texts. In the case of the king four wives are expressly mentioned. The heroes and Brahmans of the epic are frequently represented as having several wives. In addition to wives, concubines were also kept who were not married in due form, and who could not become their husbands' heirs.

To the Persians, religion offered a premium on the plurality of wives. In the absence of any fixed rule in the Zend-Avesta as to the number of wives a man might possess, they indulged in a multitude of regular matrimonial connections, besides having a number of concubines.

Among the Athenians, the most civilized and cultured nation of antiquity, the wife was a mere chattel marketable and transferable. She was regarded as an evil indispensable for the procreation of children.

The religious laws of antiquity did not place any restriction on the number of wives a man could have. The Old Testament permits polygamy without any limit. Almost all the Biblical prophets, with the exception of Christ who did not marry at all, were polygamous. King Solomon had as many as seven hundred wives and three hundred concubines. Even Jesus Christ never uttered a word against polygamy. On the other hand, eminent Christian theologians like Luther, Melanchton, Bucer, etc., did not hesitate to deduce the legality of polygamy from the parable of the ten virgins spoken of in the Gospel of Matthew, for Jesus envisages the possibility of the marriage of one man with as many as ten girls simultaneously. The Talmud restricted the number on the consideration of husband's ability to maintain wives.

Polygamy was legally practised and accepted by the Church in the Middle Ages. In the middle of the sixteenth century, Diarmait, King of Ireland, had two queens and two concubines. In later times, Philip of Hesse and Frederick William II of Prussia contracted polygamous marriages with the sanction of the Lutheran clergy. In 1650, soon after the Peace of Westphalia, when the population had been greatly reduced by the Thirty Years' War, the Frankish Kriegstag (War Parliment) at Nuremberg passed the resolution that thenceforth every man should be allowed to marry two women.[5]

Similarly, the pre-Islamic Arabs also practised polygamy without any limit. It is said that Ghaylan al-Thaqafi had ten wives when he embraced Islam.

Islamic Stand on Polygamy

When Islam came, it considerably limited the scope of polygamy. It also humanised this institution and made it conditional and purposeful. Contrary to popular belief, Islam discouraged the practice of polygamy in normal conditions by initiating various measures. Of all the religions Islam alone restricted the maximum number of wives one can possess to four. That must have been considered a great revolutionary step in those days.

Secondly, Islam enjoins upon the polygamous Muslim male to deal equitably between his wives. This is a very difficult job indeed. In case of his failure to do so he is commanded to content with only one wife as described above.

Prophet Muhammad has also warned his followers against the consequences of inequitable dealing between his wives in the following words:

"من كانت له امرأتان فلم يعدل بينهما جاء يوم القيامة وشقه ساقط"[6]

(If a person, having two wives, does not deal equitably between them, he will be raised on the

Day of Judgement with one half of his body paralyzed.)

Thirdly, the woman is given the right of separation from her husband in case he chooses to go in for a second wife without obtaining her consent. She can also claim her own establishment in that case. It therefore, does not matter much, from her point of view, whether monogamy or polygamy should be the prevailing order of society. Moreover, polygamy is permissible only when both the first wife and the prospective second wife consent to such a way of life. There is nothing in the Islamic law which can force a woman to enter into a marriage contract against her will. If she refuses to marry a man who has already one wife, she cannot be forced to become a "co-wife". As far as the first wife is concerned, she can compel her husband to remain monogamous if she so desires by laying down in the document of the marriage contract a condition to this effect. Such a condition is as valid as any other condition of a legal contract.[7]

And last but not the least, it runs counter to the Islamic spirit of social justice and universal brotherhood of mankind that some privileged and well-to-do Muslims should procure or lure more than one wife keeping thereby the less privileged and poor brethren deprived of the opportunity of having even a single wife in case of man-woman ratio in their society being about fifty-fifty. The very idea of polygamy under such conditions would go against the lofty ideals preached by Islam.

Islamic Polygamy

Although, various measures have been taken by Islam to contain polygamy within as limited a compass as possible, yet there is clear-cut provision for it in this religion in order to meet certain specific needs of society. For example, the interests of women rendered widowed and destitute following wars in which large numbers of men are killed cannot be protected by monogamy. Hence, the provision for polygamy in Islam to provide sustenance, protection and companionship to such women who might otherwise remain helpless and emotionally dissatisfied. For instance, after the battle of Uhud, when many men were killed, there was a large number of widows. Poligamy was encouraged to give protection to the helpless widows. Another important advantage of this measure was that it prevented problems of immorality that might have resulted from the presence of a large number of widows. Thus, polygamy was found to be a better alternative than secret association with women. This shows that the Islamic law on it is more elastic and more in harmony with the requirements of society than the other systems of law which preclude polygamy.

Besides, it calls for a great deal of sacrifice and responsibility on the part of the polygamous male as he is required to provide protection and sustenance to helpless women. The example of Prophet Muhammad himself is a sufficient proof in support of this point. Till the age of fifty-two he had only one wife, Khadijah, who was fifteen years senior to him. After her death he contracted a number of marriages. Except for Aishah, all his wives were widows. He married them not because he had the slightest desire for them, but in order to provide them with a home and a position they could not otherwise enjoy. For instance, Umme Salma was well advanced in age and had a number of children when her husband died in the battle of Uhud. She was left helpless without any resources to support her. It was totally out of sympathy for her as well as in recognition of the supreme sacrifices made by her husband that the Prophet married her. His remaining marriages were also motivated by similar considerations. This shows that by being polygamous he was not satisfying his lust but acting as a reformer. Thus, the Islamic polygamy is more of a social responsibility. This establishes the fact that Islam does not give anyone the licence to enjoy the luxury of plurality of wives in the garb of polygamy.

It is worthy of mention in this context that the advantages of the humanised form of polygamy as retained by Islam are best realised even by modern women living in societies where men are outnumbered by women. It is not surprising to know that African delegates to Forum 85, held at Nairobi in July 85, to assess accomplishments of the women's decade 1975-85 and to formulate strategies for their future development, frankly admitted the importance and relevance of polygamy in the following words:

"In Kenya alone, and that can hold true for other parts of Africa also, the man woman ratio is one to three-and-a half or four. Our society looks down upon single women. Women do not mind being the second, third or even the fourth wife instead of remaining single in a hostile society. Ninety per cent of our men are either killed protecting the honour of the country or are still involved in fighting. We have to manage with whatever number is left with us. How can monogamy help our interests?"[8]

If history can be any guide, enforcement of monogamy under such circumstances is bound to create many problems including illegitimate child and misery and shame for the mother. While such instances in the West are numerous, Muslim societies are almost free from this social evil.

Moreover, strict monogamy has never really been observed in Western lands. The practice of unavowed polygamy has already caused a lot of misery and hardship to countless women and children in the West. At one stage England was compelled to give indirect countenance to polygamy by recognising "war babies".

Although, various measures were taken to protect the interests of such babies by providing "Houses of Rescue" and "Foundling Hospitals", they could not be spared the ignominy that stigmatized their whole life and left their mothers in the lurch. They could have been easily saved from all this if the mothers had been allowed by the law to hold the honourable position of a second wife.[9]

From what is described above, it is quite clear that the trend of Islamic teachings is towards monogamy. Islam does not enjoin polygamy. It only recommends it in certain circumstances as better than leaving women helpless and without protectors. It can even dispense with this institution without affecting its tenets, should circumstances so dictate.

References

1. M.M. Pickthall, *op.cit.*, p. 79.
2. *Ibid.*, p. 91.
3. 'S. Ameer Ali: *The Spirit of Islam*, p. 229.
4. M.M. Pickthall, *op.cit.*, p. 91.
5. Mohammad Wassel in *Hamdard Islamicus*, Vol. VII, No. 3, p. 42.
6. محمد فريد وجدى: المبررات العلمية لمبدأ تعدد الزوجات فى الاسلام، مجلة، نور الاسلام' المجلد الخامس، ص 529
7. Mohammad Wassel, *op.cit.*, p. 42.
8. The Times of India, New Delhi, August 11, 85, p. 3.
9. Khwaja Kamaluddin: *The Ideal Prophet*, p. 150.

6

Islamic Approach to Abolition of Slavery

Some Western critics base their severest attack on Islam on account of its having tolerated and retained the institution of slavery which is considered to be a blot on the history of mankind. They, being totally ignorant and neglectful of Islamic teachings in this regard, maintain that had Islam come as a final dispensation to whole mankind, it would have abolished slavery outright. They even indict Islam of having been instrumental and responsible for the continuance of this inhuman institution in society. An instance of their biased accusation is quoted below:

> "Seeing that Mohammad himself has no scruple to own and sell his fellow men as slaves, how can we wonder that slavery has always been a recognised institution throughout the Mohammedan world? It is but natural that the religion of such a prophet should be as tolerant and favourable to the continuance of slavery as the religion of Jesus Christ tends surely, though perhaps slowly, to bring about the cessation of this degraded condition of humanity".[1]

But an impartial and comprehensive analysis of the subject clearly establishes the fact that there could not have been a better solution of this problem then that offered and practised by Islam over fourteen hundred years ago. It is important to note that there is not even a single statement in the Qur'an and in the *Sunnah* of the Prophet which may even be remotely construed to permit Muslims to perpetuate slavery. On the contrary, the numerous texts in both sources inspire Muslims to take practical measures to liberate slaves.

Origins and Growth of Slavery

Slavery is an ancient worldwide institution which is primarily a sequence of war. In remote primitive times the adult males among the enemy were killed, while the women and children were enslaved. Then, there come a time when the victor realised that a live prisoner was after all better than a dead one. Henceforth, the victors started enslaving the overpowered enemies in order to exploit them to their comfort and convenience. In view of this fact it may fairly be said that slavery marks a humanitarian improvement in the laws of war. This put a sufficient check on the vindictive passions of the conquerors in the moment of victory, which hitherto had resulted in the massacre of the prisoners-of-war. Hence, the utility and indispensability of this institution until a no-war state is finally reached by following the principles of universal brotherhood and peaceful co-existence-the two supreme objectives of Islam.

The institution which was a necessary step in human progress in early ages, was in its more cruel forms in later times the cause of an enormous amount of suffering to the slaves. The Indians, the Egyptians the Babylonians, the Greeks and the Romans—they all practised worst forms of slavery. The condition of slaves was very pitiable under them. They were regarded as a sub-human species, treated as a mere chattel and considered the absolute property of their masters, possessing no individual rights and enjoying no legal protection. The owners had unlimited rights including the power of life and death to deal with the slaves as thought fit. Besides, they were kept in chains, given harsh treatment, tortured and killed on their slightest negligences. And the people were not at all moved at the harsh treatment meted out to the slaves, simply because they considered them to be a wretched lot meant to be pressed into their service like animals. In short, they were not included among human beings. Even philosophers like Plato and Aristotle despised them. They held that the slaves should be kept deprived of civil rights. For example, Aristotle dehumanised slaves, saying:

> "A slave is a living instrument, and an instrument a lifeless slave".[3]

An idea of cruelties perpetrated on slaves by the Greeks may be had from the fact that Spartan youths were trained on how to torture and kill enemies on the persons of slaves standing unarmed in groups. Thus, a large number of slaves were tortured and killed without any justification.

Likewise, slavery was the worst abuse of the Roman Empire. Hideous crimes were committed against slaves who had no rights of body or soul against their owners. They were subjected to dredful punishments including mutilation of the nose and ears and gouging out of the eyes.[4]

It is surprising that the two major religions, Judaism and Christianity, did nothing significant to improve the conditions of slaves. Jewish legislation refused to slaves all title to independent property. Their rabbis held that whatever the slave had acquired was the property of his master.[5]

Similarly, there is no explicit condemnation of slavery in the teachings of Christianity. It was more concerned with the rights of the masters than with amelioration of the lot of slaves. Although it gives the impression of having tended to make slavery milder, it never thought of abolishing it. On the contrary, owing to its excessive care for the rights of the masters, it became instrumental in perpetuating what would have otherwise passed away.[6]

Islamic Solution to the Problem of Slavery

When Islam came and looked at the position of slaves from various angles, it did not think it proper to abolish slavery at one stroke. While dealing with this subject two important points need to be taken into consideration. First, although Islam retained the institution of slavery, it took all possible measures for its total abolition. Secondly, it humanised this institution to such an extent that slavery as retained by it is altogether different from that as practised in the pre-Islamic days.

It would be no exaggeration to say that slavery as practised in pre-Islamic days, reducing slaves as a sub-human species, was not only disapproved of by Islam, but also abolished forthwith, while the adequately modified and humanised form of slavery, elevating slaves to the status of fellow human beings, was retained by it to deal with the only unavoidable source of slavery recognised by Islam-*i.e.*, the prisoners-of-war, for all other prevalent sources of this institution such as procurement of slaves by brigandage or by any other means were banned by it outright

It is pertinent to note in this context that there is no Islamic injunction for permanent enslavement of even prisoners-of-war. The only Qur'anic verse touching upon their fate reads as follows:

"And afterwards either set them free as a favour or let them ransom themselves until the war lays down its weapons".[7]

Restoration of Human Status to the Slaves

Islam had full understanding of the human nature and psychology. It fully knew that slavery could not be abolished overnight by merely passing a legislation to that effect. Any abrupt abolition of slavery could have created more problems than solved, as happened in America following declaration of slavery as officially abolished by Abraham Lincoln with the stroke of a pen.

In order to avoid the consequences of any hasty and unimaginative action with regard to abolition of slavery, Islam launched a systematic campaign against enslavement of human beings. The first step which it took in this direction was restoration of human status to the slaves by laying down that they are the same flesh and blood who deserve humane treatment as well as deliverance from the yoke of all forms of slavery and serfdom. This is in complete contrast to the ancient practice of slavery, which sought to justify perpetual humilation of slaves by maintaining that by birth they are an inferior race. Secondly, Islam enjoined its followers to treat slaves as their brothers, as they were all descendants of Adam. It further stressed that no person should claim superiority over his slave merely on account of being his master. As described above, it recognised only one basis of superiority and nobility, *i.e.*, piety.[9]

Humane Treatment of Slaves by Masters

Islam commanded the masters to be good and fair in their dealings with the slaves. After the prohibition of idolatry the second most important law of Islam enjoins doing good to the servants of Allah including this oppressed class of human beings known as slaves.[10] This is clearly borne out by the following Qur'anic verse:

> "And serve Allah. Ascribe nothing as partner unto Him. Show kindness unto parents, and unto near

> kindred, and orphans, and the needy and the slaves whom your right hands possess."[11]

Here it is worthy of mention that the prisoners of war also had a right to kind treatment in Islam. This should be clear from the fact that even the captives at Badr were kindly treated by the Prophet, although they deserved the severest punishment as they had persecuted the Muslims most severely in Mecca. This attitude of Muslims has been applauded by Allah in the following verses:

> "And (they) feed with food the needy wretch, the orphan and the prisoner, for love of Him, saying: We feed you, for the sake of Allah only. We wish for no reward nor thanks from you."[12]

Next, the relationship between masters and slaves was based on the principles of brotherhood rather than those of slavery and overlordship. The former were held responsible for the well-being of the latter. They were asked to feed and clothe them as they did themselves. The Prophet admonished his followers to treat them with kindness in the following words:

> "Your slaves are your brothers. So, he who has a brother under him should feed and clothe him as he feeds and clothes himself. He should not ask him to do works beyond his capacity; and if he asks him to do such works, he should assist him personally."[13]

The Prophet had such kind regards for the slaves that he asked his followers not to hurt their feelings in any way. He commanded them to address their slaves in a pleasing manner instead of calling them as such. He said:

> "None of you should say: This is my slave and this is my slave-girl; he should rather say: This is my boy and this is my girl."[14]

Liberation of Slaves

Islam was not satisfied with mere restoration of human status to the slaves. In its efforts to completely wipe out slavery from society, it became the first to initiate the movement of emancipating them in a phased manner. It sought to bring about their total freedom by two important means—(1) voluntary emancipation of slaves by their masters called *al-'Itq* and (2) purchase of freedom by slaves called *mukatabah*.

Voluntary Emancipation of Slaves

Islam encouraged emancipation of slaves by describing it as an act of great piety. The Qur'an recommended their emancipation by calling it as one of such virtuous acts that make man transcendent and lead him nearer to Allah by holding it as a sign of spiritual ascent. "What is spiritual ascent? It is to redeem a slave".[15] The Prophet Muhammad also urged his followers to emancipate slaves, saying:

> "Nothing pleases Allah better than to free a slave."

> "He who sets free a Muslim slave, shall be freed from the fires of hall."

Besides, liberation of slaves is prescribed as atonement for the killing of a believer or for the breaking of an oath or for other religious and moral lapses on the part of the masters. Consider, for example, the following verses:

> "He who hath killed a believer by mistake must set free a believing slave, and pay the blood-money to the family of the slain."[16]

> "But He (Allah) will take you to task for the oaths which you swear in earnest. The expiation thereof is the feeding of ten of the needy with the average of that wherewith you feed your own folk or the

liberation of a slave."[17]

"But those who divorce
Their wives by Zihar,[18]
Then wish to go back
On the words they uttered—
It is ordained that
Such a one should free a slave
Before they touch each other;
This are ye admonished
To perform: and God is
Well-acquainted with (all)
That ye do."[19]

Furthermore, ill-treatment of slaves by their masters also leads to their liberation. This is ordered by Prophet Muhammad in the following words.

"Whosoever beats his slave, he should set him free as atonement for his beating."

"If anyone curses his slave by invoking the disgrace of Allah on him, the latter is free."

Large numbers of slaves achieved their freedom through these voluntary means of emancipation. The Prophet himself encouraged the practice of freeing slaves by setting free all the slaves he had. His Companions also followed his example. Even in the initial years of nascent Islam in Mecca where atmosphere was quite incongenial for the Muslims, Khadijah, the Prophet's wife, Abu Bakr and other wealthy Muslims freed a good number of slaves by purchasing them from the Meccan disbelievers.

The movement of freeing slaves was further accelerated following the Prophet's migration to Medina. Among the numerous Companions who distinguished themselves by liberating slaves, mention may be made of Abdullah Bin 'Umar and Abdul Rahman Bin 'Awf who set free one thousand and thirty thousand slaves respectively.[20] Similarly, Hakim Bin Hazzam, who professed Islam on the day Mecca was conquered, celebrated his profession of Islam by freeing one hundred slaves.[21]

Purchase of Freedom Called Mukatabah

The second important means, through which Islam brought freedom to slaves was that of *mukatabah, i.e.,* buying oneself free, on the basis of which the slaves could seek freedom from their masters on the payment of ransoms. This was a contractual liberation, in which the slave paid his owner a certain equivalent for his freedom. This contract could not be cancelled by the owner, while the slave could annul it if he so desired.

Furthermore, if a slave offered to ransom his freedom, his owner could neither turn down the offer, nor could he delay his emancipation on receipt of the ransom-money. Thus, by this provision Islam paved the way for the freedom of all slaves desiring liberty at their own convenience.

It was also considered virtuous to help the slave in his efforts to obtain freedom. The master was enjoined not to exact the whole amount earned by the slave; and the Qur'an has provided for a part of the *zakat* (poor-tax) to be set aside for the benefit of slaves aspiring to purchase their freedom. For example, the following Qur'anic verse lays down that a part of the poor-tax should be spent for ransoming such slaves as were unable to obtain their liberty with their own earnings:

"Alms are only for the poor and the needy, and the officials appointed over them and for the ransoming of captives."[22]

It is clear from the above that the financial assistance provided to the slaves by the state out of the Public Exchequer for the purpose of setting them at liberty was a sure manifestation of the great interest taken by Islam in the eradication of slavery.

Yet another Islamic measure which hastened the process of withering away of the institution of slavery was that, while elsewhere a child born in slavery would always remain a slave, the Prophet enjoined that if a captive or bondswoman bore a child to her master, the child would be a free child and the mother would become free.[23]

The Actual Position of Slaves in Islam

That Islamic solution to the problem of slavery was ideal and exemplary is best seen in the practical aspects of slavery as lived by slaves under the care and protection of their Muslim masters. As described above, they were given such a kindly and humane treatment that they lived as family members with their masters, enjoying thereby a status similar to that of free men. That was the main reason why many of them, even when freed by their masters, preferred to live with them instead of bidding them farewell, although now as free men they stood in no need or fear of them.

The slaves were hardly distinguishable from their masters in the practical life. Numerous examples can be cited in support of this point. Here, it would suffice to mention that when on the fall of Jerusalem Caliph 'Umar was invited to personally conclude a treaty with the notables of that city, he started his journey on a camel accompanied by a slave with the arrangement that they would ride and walk alternately. And as they approached their destination, it was the slave's turn to ride, while the caliph himself walked along.

On another occasion when Caliph 'Umar saw that a group of slaves were standing, not eating along with their masters, he became angry, reprimanded the masters for discrimination, and asked the slaves to eat along with them.

Besides, such distinguished Companions as Uthman, Abd al-Rahmen Bin 'Awf, Salman al-Farisi, etc., took pains to demonstrate perfect equality with their slaves. It is said that Uthman Bin 'Affan once rubbed up the ear of one of his slaves on a fault made by the latter. But he became so much repentant that he asked his slave to pinch his own ear in a similar manner. When the slave refrained from it, he insisted on it and got his ear pinched by him, saying: "Rub up my ear as I had done yours, for I cannot bear its punishment on the Day of Judgement". Similarly, whenever 'Abu al-Rahmen Bin 'Awf walked in the company of his slaves, it was difficult to distinguish him from his slaves as he would always clothe himself like them as well as walk in their midst rather than lead them. Again, when a certain man was once surprised to see Selman al-Farsi knead flour, the latter replied, saying that since he had already assigned a work to his servant, he did not want to task him two works.[24]

Since Muslim society was not race or colour conscious, liberated slaves of whatever origin were readily absorbed as equal members of the community. The history of Islam is replete with examples of slaves reaching the highest positions. For example, Bilal, a slave, was married to the daughter of Abu Bakr, while Salman al-Farsi was the key-holder of the Ka'bah. The emancipated slaves were entrusted with as prestigious offices as those of governors and military commanders. The Prophet himself appointed Zayd, his liberated slave, as commander of the Muslim army. After his death he was succeeded by his son Usamah as commander of the army which included such prominent Companions as Abu Bakr and Umar.

Another important measure which Islam took with a view to raising the standards of slaves in society was that they were provided with all opportunities of acquiring knowledge and learning. As a result, a good number of them like Salim, Bilal, Nafi and Ata, to mention only a few, excelled in their knowledge of the Qur'an and Apostolic Traditions, due to which they were exalted to the rank of Imam, perhaps the highest honorific title which a Muslim could obtain in those days.

That the slaves flourished, and were given high administrative posts under the Muslim rule is further established by the fact that once the Umayyad Caliph Hisham Bin Abdul Malik asked al-Zahri, the renowned scholar of Hadith, about the governors of different Muslim territories, and also wanted to know whether they were Arabs or non-Arabs. Al-Zahri replied that they were all freed slaves of foreign origin with the exception of one who was an Arab.[25]

Similarly, the slave-girls were trained to a high level of attainment. They could compose verses, engage in learned talk, and discuss philosophy and literature. All these factors greatly increased their status in society.

Thus, looking to the socially elevated position of the slaves, their treatment on a footing of equality with the masters, strict restrictions against harsh treatment and provisions of voluntary and obligatory emancipation of slaves, it would be no exaggeration to say that Islam still remains unsurpassed in securing freedom for slaves and bondsmen as well as in making them useful members of society. In practice, the Muslim bondsmen were not slaves, but captives of war, who were either to be ransomed or set free out of favour. Even such persons who were already kept in bondage under the old custom could not be called slaves, because they lived as members of the household with their respective masters enjoying several rights and privileges including the right of purchasing their freedom. In view of this fact, it may further be added that it is simply an abuse of the word slavery to apply it to the status of bondsmen as provided and maintained by the legislation of Islam. Needless to say that the brilliant practical and natural measures taken by Islam for kind, humane and brotherly treatment of slaves and other suppressed members of the human society as well as for abolition of the institution of slavery have no parallels even in the history of modern times marked by excessive propagation for championing the cause of human rights.

References

1. S. W. Koelle, *Mohammad and Mohammedanism*, p. 178.
2. *Encyclopaedia of Religion and Ethics*, Vol. XI, p. 597.
3. W. F. Thompson, *Practical Philosophy of the Mohammedan People*, p. 310.
4. *Encyclopaedia of Religion and Ethics*, Vol. XI, p. 604.
5. *Ibid.*, p. 604.
6. *Ibid.*, p. 604.
7. The Qu r'an, XLVII : 4.
8. *Encyclopaedia of Religion and Ethics*, Vol. XI, p. 619.
9. The Qur'an, XLIX: 13.
10. Shibli Nu'mani, *Sirat al-Nabi*, Vol. VI, pp. 219.
11. The Qur'an, IV: 36 (tr. by M. M. Pickthall).
12. The Qur'an, LXXVI: 8-9 (tr. by M. M. Pickthall).
13. Muhammad Qutb, *Islam, the Misunderstood Religion*, p. 70.

14. Muhammed Farid Wajdi; *"Al-Istirqaq 'ind al-Umam wa Fi al-Islam"* in the Journal *Nur al-Islam,* Vol. V, pp. 331.

15. The Qur'an, XC: 12.

16. The Qur'an, IV: 92, tr. by M. M. Pickthall.

17. The Qur'an, V: 89, tr. by M. M. Pickthall.

18. *Zihar* was the ancient pagan custom of divorcing one's wife by calling that she was just like the back of his mother for him.

19. The Qur'an, LVIII: 3, tr. by A. Yusuf Ali.

20. Shibli Nu'mani, *Sirat al-Nabi,* Vol. VI, p. 219.

21. *Ibid.,* p. 219.

22. The Qur'an, IX: 60.

23. S. Ameer Ali: "The Modernity of Islam" in the *Islamic Culture Golden Jubilee Commemoration Volume,* p. 17.

24. Dr. Salih Bin 'Abdullah : *"Mawqif al-Islam min al-Riqq"* in *Sawt al-Ummat,* Jamia Salafia, Varanasi, Vol. XXVII, No. 1 (Jan., 1995), pp. 28-29.

25. Muhammad Farid Wajdi : *"Al-Istirqaq 'ind al-Arab wa fi al-Islam"* in the journal *Nur al-Islam,* Vol-V, p. 334.

7

TREATMENT OF ANIMALS IN ISLAM

Perhaps, animals are the worst victims of the Western materialistic civilization. They are being subjected to a lot of cruelty in the name of science. Experiments on live animals in laboratories have become a major source of cruelty to them these days. In Britain alone, 4,600,000 experiments were performed in the year 1980, according to its home office statistics. The Netherlands and Sweden use one million animals each and every year. Japan has outdone Europe and uses about twenty million animals in a year. The United States of America is far ahead of the world in this field also. About sixty-three million animals die annually in its laboratories.[1]

The greatest justification for experiments on live animals has come from medicine. It is claimed that these experiments have increased man's medical knowledge and his surgical skill. Even if this justification is admitted, vivisection is neither necessary nor desirable except in very rare cases for exclusively medical purposes. Nevertheless even this justification has been challenged by sensitive people all over the world. As a result, anti-vivisection societies have come into being in many countries. They rightly argue that animals have yielded more information about themselves and about man himself to those who have gone to them in simple friendliness. They further hold that some of the greatest discoveries, even in the medical field, have been made by methods other than that of the knife. Take, for example, pulsereading which is based on the knowledge of the deeper working of the body as a system; or take acupuncture based on the knowledge of the life-currents in the body. No account of vivisection could give this knowledge of the anatomy of the inner system of the body.[2]

Raising another serious objection relating to the doubtful predictive value of these experiments, Dr. Leon Schwartzenbert, a famous cancer specialist, says: "Many experiments on animals are useless because they cannot be extrapolated to human beings. Different species differ in their basic metabolism; therefore, experiments valid for one species are not necessarily valid for another species."[3]

It is all the more horrifying to know that about two-thirds of these experiments are non-medical in nature. They are being performed by a new category of researchers called "behavioural scientists." They study the behaviour of animals under induced conditions of abnormal stress, shock and fear. They put them under prolonged punishments. These punishments include electric shocks.[4]

They also carry out "sensory deprivation tests," in which animals are deprived of their sense-organs like their eyes or ears to see how they behave without them. Most of the time, these tests are performed not to find out anything new but to confirm old facts. As described by George Bernard Shaw, Pavlov, after sacrificing hundreds of dogs, found out what every bitch-trainer in Europe already knew"

Besides, all new chemicals are tested on animals before they are out in the market. According to J. Clausen of Odense

University, Denmark, the American pharmaceutical industry alone used 35 million animals in 1965, out of which 60,000 were monkeys, 33,000 cats and 93,000 dogs. Most of the test-animals die within a stated period.[5]

Such colossal abuse of animals in laboratories is in striking contrast with Islamic injunctions for treating animals with kindness. One main objective of Islam for treating animals with kindness is that it seeks to make man kind-hearted towards all living creatures, humans and animals alike. Kindness is an important ingredient of the human conscience. Allah Himself is Compassionate and Kind, and wants man, His vicegerent on earth, to be kind-hearted towards all living creatures.

The ancient thinkers held that the animals were mere living tools without soul, and that they were deprived of the faculty of intelligence. This view prevailed upto the early nineteenth century when scientific researches shattered the old myth about them by estrablishing that they are endowned with the faculty of intelligence. This finding serves to strengthen one's faith in the Divine origin as well as scientific foundation of the Qur'an which has already described animals as organized and intelligent creatures in the following words:

> "There is not an animal on the earth, nor a flying creature flying on two wings, but they are peoples like unto You. We have neglected nothing in the Book. Then unto their Lord they will be gathered."[6] (VI: 38)

It has also been established by modern science that each species of animals that live together have some definite medium of communication among them. The Qur'an has preceded science in this field also by telling about the language of animals in the following words:

> "And Solomon was David's heir. And he said: O mankind Lo! we have been taught the language of birds....[7] (XXVII : 16)

The Qur'an has further clarified this point by ascribing speech to ants as given below:

> "Till, when they reached the Valley of the Ants, an ant exclaimed: O ants! Enter your dwellings lest Solomon and his armies crush you, unperceiving." (XXVII: 18)

Earlier, the above Verse was taken for a mere smile or a kind of metaphor. Its real significance was realised only after entomologists unravelled the ingenious and organised ways of the life of ants as well as the astounding feats they perform.

It is of course, true that man is made master of the universe. He is authorised to press into his service all the living creatures like all other objects of nature. They are all created to serve him. Allah says:

> "Have they not seen how We have created for them of Our handiwork the cattle, so that they are their owners, And have subdued them unto them so that some of them they have for riding, some for food?
>
> Benefits and drinks have they from them. Will they not then give thanks?"[9] (XXXVI: 71-73)

But man is not at all permitted by virtue of his exalted position in the universe either to ill-treat the animals or to task them beyond their capacity, for that would amount to an act of *israf* (wantonness), which he is forbidden to practise in his life under all circumstances.

Prophet Muhammad (peace be on him) who was sent as "a mercy for the peoples" was full of kindness for the animals also. He could not tolerate even the slightest sign of cruelty to them. He forbade the pre-Islamic practice of cutting tales and manes of horses, of branding animals on any soft spot, and of keeping horses saddled unnecessarily. If he saw an animal ill-fed or overburdened, he would admonish the owner, saying: "Fear Allah in your treatment of animals."

The Noble Prophet was so full of care for the animals that he commanded his followers to cause the least possible pain to them even at the time of slaughtering them. Shaddad bin Aws has reported the Prophet as saying: "Allah has commanded you to show kindness to everyone, so if you have to kill, kill nicely, and if you slaughter an animal, slaughter it gently. If anyone of you has to slay an animal, he should sharpen the blade first and treat the animal well."[10]

On another occasion, when a man threw a goat on its side and then started sharpening his knife, the Holy Prophet (peace be on him) said: "Do you want to kill it twice? Why did you not sharpen the knife before throwing it on the ground."[11]

The Noble Prophet (peace be on him) further asked his followers to refrain from causing any disturbance or harassment to the animals. A number of instances can be mentioned where he reprimanded them for causing annoyance to animals just for fun. It is related that a certain companion came to him with the young ones of a bird in his sheet and said that he had picked them from a bush, and that the motherbird had hovered over them all along. He was directed to put back her offspring in the same bush immediately.[12] Again, when his army marched towards Mecca to conquer it.

they passed by a bitch with puppies. The Noble Prophet (peace be on him) not only gave orders that they should not be distrubed, but also posted a man to ensure that this was done. He has also forbidden the shooting of tied or confined animals and beating them on the face.[14] It is worthy of mention that he took care to save animals not only from physical cruelty, but also from all sorts of psychological injury and mental torture. Consider, for example, the following saying of the Noble Prophet (peace be on him) :

> "When you travel in a fertile country, do not deny the camels their due from the ground, and when you travel in a land barren and dry, cover it with speed. When you encamp at night, keep away from the roads, for they are where the beasts pass and are the resorts of the insects at night.[15]

Another important measure taken by Islam to curb cruelty to animals is that it holds man accountable for his treatment of them in the hereafter also. As described by the Prophet, a woman was thrown into the hell only because she neither gave food and water to a cat which she had kept tied, nor did she set it free so that it might satisfy its hunger by catching worms and insects.[16]

On the other hand, showing kindness and doing good to animals have been described by Islam as meritorious acts of virtue that may earn man pleasure of Allah. The Prophet has elaborated this point, saying: "While on his way, a traveller felt thirsty. He saw a well, descended into it and quenched his thirst. When he came out, he saw a dog lolling its tongue and licking the moist earth because of thirst. He became sure that it felt the same intensity of thirst as he had felt himself. So he got into the well again, filled his leather sock with water, came out carrying it with his teeth, and quenched the thirst of the dog. Allah was pleased with him and pardoned his sins." Hearing this his companions asked him if there was some reward for them in the matter of beasts and wild animals also. He told them that there was a reward for them for their kind treatment of every living creature.[17]

From what precedes it is quite clear that Islam has taken all possible measures not only to curb cruelty to animals, but also to treat them kindly and gently. Besides developing in man the humane qualities of kindness and compassion for the living creatures, these measures also serve to maintain the ecological balance to the advantage of mankind by letting different species of animals, birds and insects grow and prosper in an atmosphere congenial to them.

References

1. Ram Swarup: "Cruelty to Animals," published in the *Times of India,* New Delhi, June 26, 1986.
2. *Ibid.*
3. *Ibid.*
4. The Times of India, *op. cit.,* dated June 27,1986.
5. *Ibid.*
6. M.M. Pickthall: *The Meaning of the Glorious Koran,* p. 111.
7. *Ibid.,* p. 273.
8. *Ibid.*
9. *Ibid.,* p. 318.
10. Abul Hasan Ali al-Nadwi: *Muhammad Rasulullah,* p. 437.

11. *Ibid.*, p. 438.
12. Athar Husain: *Prophet Muhammad and his Mission*, p. 145.
13. *Ibid.*, p. 146.
14. *Sahih Bukhari.*
15. *Muhammad Rasulullah, op. cit.*, p. 439.
16. Narrated by al-Bukhari.
17. Narrated by al-Bukhari.

8

Islam and Science

Islam is not at all a dogmatic religion confined to the four walls of the mosque, but rather it is a natural and scientific way of living which aims at full flowering of all the spiritual, mental and other inherent faculties, with which Allah, the Creator, has endowed man, giving him the status of being the noblest creature in the universe. It came to give man confidence in his own destiny by clarifying that he was created to worship Allah and act as His vicegerent on earth, and that everything else was created to serve him. It also cancelled the past based on superstitions and false notions. This was undoubtedly an unparalleled revolution brought about on earth in the domain of scientific knowledge and learning.

Islam inspired man to unravel the secrets of nature more than any other school of thought could do with the two-fold purpose of doing welfare to humanity at large as well as making him believe in the existence of Almighty Allah, because the more he knows about the universe, the more conscious he is likely to become of the Creator of the universe, provided of course he is equipped with a sound reasoning power. This is clearly expressed in the Qur'an in the following words:

"It is scholars among His servants who fear Allah Alone. Lo! Allah is Mighty Forgiving".[1]

The above Verse makes it quite clear that acquisition of knowledge and learning is an essential condition for man to become a purposeful and sincere servant of Allah. In other words, it is required that he must apply his intellect and power of observation, instead of superstitions and false notions, in his comprehension and appreciation of the manifestations of nature to be able to feel in his heart and mind the immensity and greatness of the Wisdom, Might, Knowledge and Crative Power of Allah.

It is with the explicit purpose of instilling in man the spirit of becoming scientific and rational that Islam has put the greatest possible emphasis on the pursuit of knowledge and learning. It is described as one of the unavoidable injunctions of Allah that are incumbent upon man. That is the main reason why cultivation of knowledge is regarded in Islam as a sacred work of worship to Allah.

Both the Qur'an and Traditions of Prophet Muhammad, the two main sources of Islamic thought, are full of such expressions as emphasize the importance of knowledge in the life of man on the one hand and stimulate him to cultivate it on the other. A brief account of such Qur'anic Verses is given below in support of this point.

It is important to note in this context that Allah has clearly highlighted the dignity of the high office of knowledge by making Adam superior to the angels. The angels were ordered to prostrate themselves before Adam only after it was demonstrated that they possessed less knowledge than that granted to the latter.[2]

Besides, a number of the early Verses of the Qur'an were revealed to raise the banner of knowledge. The very first five Verses revealed to the Prophet commanded him to read and learn:

> "Read in the name of thy Lord Who created; created man from a clot. Read: And thy Lord is the most Bounteous Who taught by the pen. Taught man that which he knew not."[3]

At another place Allah has highlighted the value and dignity of the pen by swearing by it, while upholding the lofty character of Prophet Muhammad :

> "Nun and by the pen and whatever they write, you are not by the grace of your Lord a madman".[4]

Allah's swearing by the pen in those days and particularly among the Arabs who always boasted of the sword and attached little importance to the pen, being ignorant of it, might have sounded strange and insignificant. But now history has proved beyond any shadow of doubt that the pen is mightier than the sword. Today nobody denies it.

Likewise, there are numerous other Qur'anic Verses and Apostolic Traditions that emphasize upon the followers of Islam the importance of knowledge and learning for success in this life and in the hereafter.[5] It is worth mentioning in this context that there is nothing in the Qur'an which does not appeal to reason and intellect. It has ordained various measures to enable man to promote his scientific outlook, critical acumen and intellectual capacity for a better perception of the surroundings around him. First, it gives man tremendous self-confidence in his own destiny by telling him in clear terms that he is the supreme creature in the universe, and that all other things including the stars, the sun, the moon, the animal kingdom, the plant kingdom, etc., are created to serve him.

As such he is exhorted to conquer the universe and press it into the service of humanity at large. Secondly, the Qur'an seeks to purge the human mind of all sorts of superstitions, delusions and prejudices that kill its vitality. It has denounced conjecture, illusion and empty guesswork in the following words :

> "And they have no knowledge thereof. They follow but a guess, and a guess can never take the place of the truth."[6]

> "And they say: If the Beneficent One had so willed, we should not have worshipped them. They have no knowledge whatsoever of that. They do but guess".[7]

It is clear from the above Verses that Islam does not permit blind imitation of unhealthy traditions inherited from others, even from one's own parents.

Thirdly, man is repeatedly asked in the Qur'an to assert his reason and intellect to attain knowledge. This is evident from the fact that the word *ilm* (knowledge) and its derivatives have occurred 805 times; the word *albab* (minds) has occured 16 times; and the word *aql* (reason) and its derivatives have occured 49 times in the Qur'an.[8]

Fourthly, the Qur'an exhorts time and again to observe and investigate natural phenomena with a view to getting acquainted with the Laws of Nature. About 750 Verses of the Qur'an-almost one-eighth of the Book-emphasize reflection on natural phenomena with examples drawn from cosmology, physics, biology and medicine.[9] Consider, for example, the following Verses:

> "Do they not look
>
> At the sky above them?

How We have made it
And adorned it,
And there are no Flaws in it?
And the earth—
We have spread it out
And set thereon mountains
Standing firm, and produced
Therein every kind of
Beautiful growth (in pairs)
To be observed
And commemorated
By every devotee
Turning (to God).[10]
Do they not look at the camels,
How they are made ?
And at the Sky,
How it is raised high?
And at the Mountains,
How they are fixed firm?
And at the Earth,
How it is spread out?[11]

Obviously, the call for observing the natural phenomena as embodied in the above Verses does not mean mere casting a superficial look at them, but rather it is implied that man should try to ascertain the universal laws of Nature operating in them by developing and applying the experimental method of research based on all the faculties of reason and perception, with which he has been endowed by Allah. Otherwise,in the event of his failure to do so, he is condemned as worse than cattle that have hearts wherewith they understand not, eyes wherewith they see not, and ears wherewith they hear not.[12]

Yet another important method taught by the Qur'an to facilitate the search for scientific knowledge is the process of comparing and investigating the pattern of creation in different objects of Nature :

> "And two seas (*i.e.*, the two kinds of water in the earth) are not alike: this, fresh, sweet, good to drink, this (other) bitter, salt. And from them both ye eat fresh meat and derive the ornament that ye wear".[13]

By referring to various objects of Nature and natural phenomena, the Qur'an not only stirred man's intellectual curiosity, but also greatly advanced his scientific knowledge about the universe. There are a number of passages in the Book that catapulted man to the utmost heights of scientific knowledge by disclosing some secrets of Nature which science has taken hundreds of years to verify and establish. Consider, for example, the following Verse, in which the Qur'an teaches man pure science by alluding to the rotation of the earth and other celestial bodies :

> "And He it is Who created the night and the day, and the sun and the moon. They float, each in an orbit".[14]

Secondly, fertilization of trees by winds has only recently been discovered by science, to which the Qur'an has referred in the following words:

"And We send the winds fertilizing".[15]

Similarly, the production of water from the clouds through the process of fertilization of the positive and negative electric charges is vividly and precisely described in the Qur'an as follows :

> "Seest thou not that God makes the clouds move gently, then joins them together, then makes them into a heap, then wilt thou see rain issue forth from their midst?"[16]

The Qur'an is full of such scientific miracles. A few more instances of the miraculous nature of the Book from the modern scientific viewpoint are given below.

It is now fully established by science that everything exists in pairs as male and female including the rock crystals and electricity.[17] The same fact was revealed in the Qur'an as follows:

"Praise be to Him Who created all things in pairs, of that which the earth grows, and of their own kind, and of kinds which they know not".[18]

As established by geneticists, it is the sperms that are the deciding factor in determining the type of sex (male or female) in the new embryo. As per the findings of modern science, the sperms have X and Y chromosomes, while the female eggs have only Y chromosomes. The same fact is described in the Qur'an in the following words, in which the origin of man is attributed to the sperm rather than to the female egg :

> "Does man think that he will be left uncontrolled (without purpose)? Was he not a drop of sperm emitted (in lowly from) ? Then did God make and fashion him in due proportion. And of him he made two sexes, male and female. Has He not the power to give life to the dead".[19]

Another startling scientific discovery made in recent years regarding the comets of ice clearly brings to light the significance of the information contained in the following Qur'anic Verse :

> "He sendeth down from the mountains wherein is hail..."[20]

It is clear from the above Verse that mountains of ice or comets of ice are being sent down regularly from the sky (space) towards the earth. Scientists were totally ignorant of this phenomenon until 1986. It was scientifically confirmed only in 1988. According to this discovery, heavy snowballs or comets of ice weighing about 100 tons each and measuring about 30 feet across are constantly falling from unknown places from the space into the earth's atmosphere at the rate of 10 million a year. Finally, they break up into hail due to tidal waves in the atmosphere, and join the earth's water cycle.[21]

It is important to note in this context that there is not even a single statement in the Qur'an dealing with natural phenomena which contradicts what is known for certain from the discoveries in modern sciences.[22] The modern scientific discoveries have, on the other hand, only added to the truthfulness of this Book by further elaborating its Verses containing scientific information. This fact is acknowledged by Maurice Bucaille in the introductory chapter of his book *The Bible, the Qur'an and Science* in the following words:

> "The Qur'an did not contain a single statement that was assailable from a modern scientific point of view".[23]

Inspired by these and like Qur'anic Verses and Apostolic Traditions, Muslims, both Arab and non-Arab, were filled with the spirit of scientific enquiry. Having thus developed a keen sense of intellectual curiosity and a voracious appetite for learning, they travelled far and wide in search of knowledge, and contributed a great deal to human thought and progress by pursuing and patronising study and research in all branches of learning with a view to promoting the welfare of humanity at large.

The Muslims further showed signs of their intellectual awakening by providing educational facilities on a large scale. The famous Muslim capitals like Damascus, Baghdad, Cairo, Cordova, etc., became the chief centres of spreading education and conducting scientific researches. An idea of their rich intellectual legacy may be easily gained from the fact that they have left more than one million Arabic manuscripts, out of which only about one lakh manuscripts could be studied and analyzed so far, while the remaining nine lakh manuscripts are yet to see the light of day.[24] Furthermore, when misfortunes befell the Muslim world in general and the Arabs of Italy, France and Spain in particular, the most precious booty treasured by the Europeans was a large number of Arabic books and manuscripts. They collected more than 2,50,000 Arabic books and manuscripts, and decorated their libraries with theme. For instance, the libraries of Berlin, Paris, London, Leipzis, Oxford, Madrid, etc. are still very famous for possessing large numbers of rare Arabic books and manuscripts on different branches of learning cultivated by the Arabs and Muslims.[25]

The Muslims made valuable contributions to the development of natural and life sciences. The achievements made by them in exact and other sciences are also highly commendable and praiseworthy. A brief introduction to their achievements in some of these fields is attempted below as specimens of their scientific heritage, on account of which they deserve to be honoured as the main connecting link between the Greco-Roman classical age and the modern scientific era.

Medicine

The science of medicine developed a great deal at the hands of the Arabs and Muslims who cultivated it with great zeal and made spectacular achievements in almost all the branches connected with the curative science, namely, clinical treatment, pharmacy, surgery, the art of nursing patients in hospitals, ophthalmology, anatomy, psychotherapy, etc. It is they who introduced experimental methods into the study of diseases and their treatment at a time when their European counterparts looked upon some serious diseases like small-pox and epidemics as manifestations of the wrath of and punishment from God.

It should be clearly borne in mind in this context that the history of the Muslim legacy to medicine begins right from the lifetime of Prophet Muhammad (peace be upon him) himself, whose teachings brought about a revolution in the art of preserving and restoring health by laying down fundamental principles as preventive measures for the improvement of both physical and psychic hygiene.[26] It was mainly because of the various sanitary measures which were introduced by the Prophet as part of the Islamic *Shariat* that the Muslim world, so long it implemented them, was saved from the onslaught of dangerous epidemics which occured in different parts of the world killing large numbers of people.

It is noteworthy that the great plague known as the Black Death, which swept through Europe in the middle of the fourteenth century, killing one-fourth of the European population, stopped at the borders of the Muslim world because of the Islamic measures of cleanliness alone.[27]

Further, George Barnard Shaw has, in his book *The Doctor's Dilemma,* highly applauded the importance and role of the Islamic care of cleanliness in building a healthy society by describing that when Britain conquered the Muslim Sandwich Islands (now the Hawaiian Islands), it compelled the population to renounce Islam and adopt Christianity. And no sooner did it succeed in replacing Islam by Christianity than this led to outbreak of epidemic diseases in the islands, "because the formulators of the superseded native religion, like Mahomet, had been enlightened enough to introduce as religious duties such sanitary measures as ablution and the most careful and reverent treatment of everything cast off by the human body, even to nail clippings and hairs; and our missionaries thoughtlessly discredited this godly doctrine without supplying its place, which was promptly taken up by laziness and neglect".[28]

It goes to the credit of the Muslims that they started practical education for medical students in their hospitals. They were the first to require their physicians and druggists to submit to a test before they could be permitted to practise their profession. They also established asylums for the care and treatment of the insane, while such patients in the West were kept confined in chains and severely beaten.

The Muslim hospital system was organized on modern lines. There were different wards for different diseases. Each ward had a number of specialized physicians. Both physicians and paramedical personnel, like attendants, technicians and druggists, worked on shift basis, who were available in their respective wards and rooms during their duty hours. Each hospital had laboratories, dispensaries, outdoor clinics, kitchens and baths. It was equipped with a library also. The Ibn Tulun Hospital of Egypt contained more than one hundred thousand books on different subjects.

Since the hospitals served as medical schools also, each hospital had a big lecture hall, in which lectures were delivered and practical education was imparted to the students as is done today in the hospitals attached to the medical colleges. The attendance of the students was compulsory in the hospitals. The conditions and diseases of the patients were also discussed and recorded. For example, the book *al-Hawi* by al-Razi contains detailed descriptions of such clinical observations and treatments.

So much attention was paid to the care of the sleepless among the patients in some hospitals that they were provided with professional musicians, story-tellers and excellent reciters of the Qur'an. While the musicians and story-tellers entertained the patients with soft music, interesting stories and humorous anecdotes, the reciters of the Qur'an sought to stimulate their spiritual capacity with a view to solidifying their self-confidence. Besides, they were made to walk in the open air and given relaxing baths in order to mitigate their distress by relieving symptoms of tension. Of the numerous hospitals that spread throughout the Muslim world, the Adudi Hospital at Baghdad, the Nuri Hospital at Damascus, the Mansuri Hospital at Cairo and the Muwahhidi Hospital at Morocco were very famous.

The endeavours made by Muslim physicians in fighting contagious diseases were also highly commendable and praiseworthy. They discovered and successfully treated a number of contagious diseases such as leprosy, tuberculosis, small-pox, measles, scabies, epidemic plague etc. 'Ali Ibn Sahl al-Tabari was the first Muslim physician who described the disease of leprosy in detail along with its symptoms such as deformation of the fingers, wrinkling of the nails and contraction of the nose. Ibn Sina was another eminent physician who contributed a great deal to the study and treatment of this disease on scientific lines. He was also the first to give a minute description of the disease of tuberculosis, which, as described by him, mostly occured in the age group of eighteen to thirty.

The credit for accurately distinguishing between the contagious diseases of small-pox and measles goes to Ibn Zakariya al-Razi. His book *al-Judariyu w-al-Hasbah* (Small-pox and Measles) is one of the most outstanding books on this subject which was translated into Latin and other European languages, and published more than forty times between 1498 and 1866. His most comprehensive medical work *al-Hawi* in twenty volumes is too well-known to need any introduction. It was translated into Latin under the title *Continens*, and exerted a great influence on European medicine.

The Muslim physicians made successful attempts to fight the dreadful contagious disease of the plague also by describing the causes of its spread. It was clearly pointed out by the physician Lisanuddin Ibn-ul-Khatib in his book *Muqni 'at-ul-Sa 'il 'an-il-Marad-il-Ha'il* (Satisfier of the Inquirer about the Dreadful Disease) that contagious diseases spread either through contact with the patient or through that with the dresses and utensils used by him. Air was also described by him as an active agent of spreading bacteria of such diseases. In view of this fact it is wrong to say that "the first consistent explanation of the spread of disease by contagion was made by the Veronese physician Girilamo Fracastoro".[29] It is interesting to note that this Italian physician and philosopher (1478-1553 C.E.), whose work on contagious diseases is said to have greatly developed our knowledge of infectious diseases, had been a student at the medical school of Padua which was a great centre of Islamic medicine in those days.

Surgery

The Muslim contribution to surgery is best represented by Abul Qasim al-Zahrawi (936-1013 C.E.) of Muslim Spain, who was a devoted surgeon, to whom both medical students and patients flocked from all parts of Europe and the Muslim world for advice and treatment. His claim to fame rests on his medical encyclopaedia *al-Tasrif.* This book is divided into thirty sections, in the last of which he has summed up the surgical knowledge of his time. It also contains illustrations of about 200 surgical instruments, most of which the author had designed and developed himself. The surgical part of the book was early translated into Latin by Gerard of Cremona. Later, it was translated into Hebrew, French and English also. Various editions of this book were published at Venice in 1497, at Basel in 1541 and at Oxford in 1778.[30] It was considered so indispensable for medical students in those days that the famous French surgeon Guy de Chauliac (1300-1366 C.E.) appended its Latin version to his own book on surgery.

In his capacity as physician-surgeon, al-Zahrawi rendered valuable services to humanity by making numerous researches and inventions which helped lay the foundations of surgery on modern lines. He introduced such new ideas as crushing a stone inside the bladder and the necessity of vivisection and dissection. He was very expert in the treatment of wounds and accident injuries as well as in the setting of bones in both simple and compound fractures. Of the numerous other achievements made by him, he performed caesarean operations and wrote in detail about them. Oral surgery and dentistry were also highly developed by him. But it is height of either intellectual dishonesty or ignorance on the part of Western historians of medicine that some of the most original inventions of this Arab surgeon are ascribed to Western physicians and surgeons. For instance, the obstetric position known as the Walcher position after the German physician Walcher (d. 1935 C.E.) was first invented and successfully implemented by al-Zahrawi. Secondly, al-Zahrawi was also the inventor of the obstetric forceps for the sake of facilitating the task of delivery in cases of emergency.[31] The credit for this invention is wrongly given to Peter Chamberlen I (1560-1631 C.E.), physician to James I and his wife. It is said that this instrument was kept a closely guarded secret by the succeeding generations of his family for a long period of time.[32]

Ibn-ul-Quff (1233-1285 C.E.) of Egypt was another renowned Muslim surgeon. His book *Umdat-ul-Jarrahin* (Support of Surgeons), containing a comprehensive description of surgical operations and bodily injuries, was the first Arabic text exclusively devoted to the art of surgery. In it he has explained "the functions of the capillaries-the minute blood passages that connect arteries and veins-and the action of cardiac valves in the veins and in the heart chambers, describing how they open in only one direction to keep blood flowing in the same way".[33]

Anatomy

The glaring achievements of the Muslims. in the science of anatomy are generally dismissed by Western historians on the assumption that since they were forbidden by their religion to practise dissection of the human body, they could not contribute much to the progress of anatomical, physiological and surgical knowledge, and consequently medical science never went beyond Galen under them. But the fact is far from being the case, for there is nothing in Islam which may be interpreted to be a ban on the dissection of the human body for medical purposes. It is, of course, true that mutilation of the dead body is forbidden in Islam in the light of the Prophet's saying: "Refrain from mutilating the body". But that is altogether in a different context. On the contrary, Islam has drawn man's attention to his anatomical structure right from the stage of his conception in the womb to that of his delivery as a child in the words :

> "O mankind ! if ye have
>
> A doubt about the Resurrection,
>
> (Consider) that We created you
>
> Out of dust, then out of leech-like
>
> Clot, then out of a morsel
>
> Of flesh, partly formed
>
> And partly unformed, in oroer
>
> That We may manifest
>
> (Our power) to you;
>
> And We cause whom We will
>
> To rest in the wombs
>
> For an appointed term,
>
> Then do We bring you out
>
> As babes..."[34]

It is worthy of mention in this context that modern scientists have expressed their astonishment over the perfection and accuracy, with which the formation and development of the human embryo has been described in the above Qur'anic verse. The findings of Dr. Keith Moore, a University of Toronto embryologist, corroborated by the test-tube baby pioneer, Dr. Robert Edwards, reveal that the above Verse contains an accurate description of the stage by stage development of the human embryo. This idea was first proposed by Western experts only in 1940, most of which was scietifically proved only recently.[35]

Yet another Qur'anic Verse which urges man to study the formation and structure of bones and flesh in the body reads as follows :

"Look further at the bones,

How We bring them together

And clothe them with flesh".[36]

Inspired by these Qur'anic Verses, Muslim scientists thoroughly analyzed the Greek legacy to anatomy and enriched it with their own contributions. Al-Jahiz (d.868 C.E.), Yuhanna Ibn Masawayh (d. 857 C.E.), Hunayn Ibn Ishaq (d. 673 C.E.), "Ali Ibn 'Abbas (d. 994 C.E.), Abdul Latif al-Baghdadi, etc., greatly advanced our knowledge of the anatomical structure of different parts of the human body, specially the skull, the ear and the eye.

Another crowning achievement in the field of anatomy was made by Ibn-al-Nafis (1210-1288 C.E.), who served as personal physician to the Mamluk sultan, Zahir Baybars, hero of the Crusade wars. He minutely and scientifically described the lungs and the blood circulation about three centuries ahead of William Harvey, who is erroneously credited with having been the first discoverer of it. He was also the first to notice that the heart has blood vessels inside its muscles. As regards the blood circulation of the heart, it was described by the Spanish Arab physician Ibn Rushd in his *Al-Kulliyat*. In this way the Muslim scientists not only studied and assimilated the Greek legacy to anatomy, but also enriched it with their own contributions.

Psychotherapy

Psychotherapy which is usually taken to be a recently developed branch of medicine, had already been highly developed by medieval Muslim physicians. Some of them specialized in it and made a systematic study of psychological diseases and their treatment.

As in other sciences, in this branch of knowledge also the Qur'an proved an effective source of inspiration to the Muslims. It prescribes a number of measures for the betterment of the general mental and physical health of man by correcting, sharpening and busying the reflecting, meditating and imagining faculties in him on scientific and experimental lines. The entire Qur'anic teaching is aimed at initiating man into the world of light by curing him of the various causes of mental sickness that so often sap his vitality and make his life miserable.

An important point taught by Qur'an with a view to correcting the vision and outlook of man, a precondition for achieving the soundness of heart and mind, is that the Creator is all the time in a state of glory only because He is all the time Perfect Law and Perfect Justice. The terms Religion, Justice, Law and Will are used almost synonymously with one another as well as illustratively of the same Creative Reality Who alone is the sole Rewarding and Punishing Agency in the universe.

The Qur'an further teaches that man is empowered not only to correct himself and better his lot, but also to influence the state of nature on earth through his deeds and words with the aid of the guidance received by him from the Creator. In other words if a man remains manly, just, truthful, constructively hard-working, self-disciplined and sincerely faithful to the Law-giver's mission of creation, he would not only improve his own physical and mental health, but also simultaneously become a potent factor in affecting the global ecosystems to the extent of making Nature yield both seen and unseen blessings to his advantage. In short, the Qur'an develops a tremendous self-confidence in man and makes himself the architect of his destiny. Faith in this Qur'anic concept of reward and punishment serves to make him optimistic, enthusiastic and self-disciplined leading to his enlightenment by ridding him of the causes of fear and sorrow.

Inspired by the Qur'anic teachings of mental and psychological health, the Muslim physicians laid down the fundamental principles of psychotherapical treatment. Ali Bin Sahl al-Tabari (d. 861 C.E.), author of the earliest Arabic book on medicine titled *Firdaws al-Hikmah* (Paradise of Wisdom), described psychological diseases as diseases of the head that are generally caused by mental disorders consequent upon psychological factors such as grief, anger, *ishq* (love), etc. He has suggested that such diseases can be cured by removing the causes of anger and insecurity to the patient as well as by pacifying his heart with pleasant conversations congenial to his ethos.

Ishaq Bin 'Imran (d. 908 C.E.) was another eminent Muslim psychotherapist. He was also the first Muslim author, who wrote an independent book on the disease of melancholia. He elaborated in detail the psychological conditions that overtake men and women in the face of great and recurrent emotional setbacks. Side by side with treating such patients with drugs and medicines, he recommended and applied psychological methods of treatment such as their entertainment through pleasant conversections, music, gentle behaviour and sightseeing as well as massaging their bodies with soothing oils followed by their baths.

Ibn Zakariya al-Razi (d. 932 C.E.) wrote a separate book on psychotherapy under the title *al-Tibb al-Ruhani*, in which he has thrown sufficient light on the methods, scope and application of psychiatric medicine by pointing out the close relationship between psyche and soma. He revealed that even indigestion is preceded by psychological upheavals in the body. Psychological conditions, according to this physician, have always the upper hand in regulating health because the ethos of the body is governed by the impact of such conditions dominating the mind. On the basis of this argument he held that only a competent psychotherapist could become a successful physician.

Ibn Sina (d. 1038 C.E.) was another important physician, who contributed much to the development of psychotherapy. His medical encyclopaedia *the Canon* remained the supreme authority on medicine for about six centuries not only in the Muslim world, but also in the West. He was the first physician to clearly point out that much of natural disposition of the mother is diffused into her children through breast-feeding. He, therefore, advised that the breast-feeding mother should keep herself on a high level of morality for the sake of the child.

Besides, there were numerous other physicians who excelled in this branch of medical treatment. Although it is not possible to enumerate the achievements of all of them, a passing reference to the remaining eminent of them is given below.

Ibn-ul-Jazzar Ahmad Bin Ibrahim (d. 1005), author of several books, in which he disseminated his vast knowledge on psychotherapy including the management and care of children right from the moment of their conception in the womb to the stage of their adolescence; Ali Bin Ridwan (d. 1067), author of *al-Kifayah f-il-Tibb*, in which he has illustrated the point that the beating of the heart is closely related with the psychological conditions of the mind; Hibatullah Abul Barakat, who flourished in Baghdad in the twelfth century of the Christian era; Ibn Zuhr (d. 1162) of Muslim Spain; and Dawud al-Antaki (d. 1600 C.E.), to mention only a few, were eminent physicians, who have discussed a number of psychological diseases in their medical works.

Zoology and Veterinary Medicine

Islam inspired the early Muslims to develop a strong interest in the kingdom of animals by describing them as organised and intelligent creatures that deserve proper attention and kind treatment. They paid special attention to the care, feeding, breeding and scientific study of them. A number of Muslim scientists flourished who made systematic studies on animals, wrote books on them, and thus contributed a great deal to the sciences of zoology and veterinary medicine.

Al-Jahiz (d. 869 C.E.) was the first eminent Arab zoologist whose *Kitab-ul-Hayawan* was a systematic and comprehensive study on animals. In it, he has described in detail the kinds of animals, their behavioural characteristics and their diseases and treatment. This encyclopaedic work in seven big volumes, in which he has quoted and criticised Aristotle at several places, proved a very useful contribution on the history of natural science. It also contained germs of the later theories of evolution, adaptation and animal psychology.[37] The chief merit of this book lies in the fact that besides tapping almost all the extant sources of knowledge on animal life, he has provided a great deal of fresh scientific information on the subject from his own observations and experiments as well as from the discussions which he held with those who had first-hand knowledge about animals such as sailors and hunters.

The chief original contribution of al-Jahiz in this book is that he has discussed for the first time such mechanisms of biological evolution as struggle for existence, transformation of species and environmental factors. Illustrating his theory of struggle for existence, he says that there is a natural war for life between every individual existence, and that the struggle exists between the members of different as well as the same species.[38]

As regards the process of transformation of species and mutation, al-Jahiz holds that it operates in conjunction with the effect of environmental factors like food, climate, shelter, etc., and that the new characteristics thus developed help them survive their environmental conditions in a better way.[39] This theory of biological evolution has influenced a number of Muslim and European thinkers including Ibn Zekariya al-Qazwini, Kamaluddin al-Damiri, al-Biruni, al-Nuwayri, C. Linnaeus (1707-1778 C.E.), Lamarch (1744-l829 C.E.) and Darwin (1809-1882 C.E.).[40]

The Egyptian scholar Kamaluddin al-Damiri (d. 1405 C.E.) was the next eminent author on this subject. Greatly influenced by al-Jahiz, he became the greatest Arab zoologist. His book *Hayat-ul-Hayawan* (Life of the Animals), arranged in the alphabetical order, contains a mine of curious information on animal life and natural science. Al-Mas'udi, Ibn Sina, Ibn Rushd and the *Ikhwan-ul-Safa* (the Brethren of Purity) were other prominent Muslim writers who made significant contributions to zoology.

Likewise, veterinary science developed side by side with the cultivation of zoological studies. The first systematic book on this subject was written by Muhammad Bin Akhi Hizam around 860 C.E. under the title *al-Furusiyah w-al-Khayl* (Horsemanship and the Horses). It deals with the behaviour and characteristics of horses as well as their diseases and treatment. Several other books on this subject were produced by different authors, some of which contained beautiful illustrations of domestic animals.

The book *al-Mukhassas* by Ibn Sidah (d. 1066 C.E.) was another monumental contribution in this field. Written in the form of a dictionary, it discusses the characteristics of camels, goats, sheep, birds, wild animals, etc., as well as the diseases that afflict them. It also contains information about useful and harmful insects. It was printed in seventeen volumes at the Bulaq Press in Egypt.

But the greatest medieval work on veterinary science is the comprehensive manual *kamil-ul-Sina 'atayn f-il-Baytarah w-al-Zardaqah* by Abu Bakr al-Baytar (d. 1340 C.E.) of Cairo, who was incharge of the stable of the Mamluk sultan, Muhammad al-Nasir Bin Qalawun. It covers a wide range of topics including animal behaviour, husbandry, breeding, variations in wild and domestic animals, horsemanship and related matters.[41] It contains a specialized and detailed study on animal diseases in different seasons, particularly those of horses, and on the methods of their prevention and treatment with drugs. A separate chapter is devoted to the discussion of determining the age of horses with the mention of their anatomical characteristics. Divided into ten sections, this book is a voluminous work which contains the sum total of the medieval Arab knowledge of veterinary medicine.

An idea of the success achieved by the Muslims in animal husbandry and veterinary medicine may be derived from the huge quantities of animal produce under their management. The period in which the Mamluk sultan, Muhammad al-Nasir Bin Qalawun ruled was the most notable for the breeding of animals on scientific lines. The sultan was very fond of horses and cattle. He even established a farm at his castle in 714 A.H When he died in 741 A.H., there were as many as 80,000 cattle in it. Besides, as reported by al-Maqrizi, over 60,000 cattle were slaughtered annually from that farm. Similarly Sultan al-Malik al-Zahir Burquq also had a great interest in the breeding of animals. He is said to have left behind at his castle 12,000 horses, 5000 camels and an equal number of mules. That was in addition to the large numbers of cattle that were slaughtered from his farm for daily consumption.

Obviously, the fruitful breeding of domestic animals on such a wide scale could not have been possible except with the efficient services of competent veterinary physicians and skilled workers.

Botany and Agriculture

The contributions made by the Muslims in botany and agriculture are also very valuable. The Greek and Nabatean legacies together with the indigenous traditions formed the basis of their botanical and agricultural knowledge.

The Qur'an which contains about 169 references to plants not only inspired the Muslims to study plant life, but also provided them with a great deal of scientific information about it. Its description of the origin of life in general including plant life-that every living thing is created out of water[43]—is strictly in accordance with modern scientific data, according to which life is not possible without water as it is the major component of all living cells.[44]

The Qur'an further elaborates that the vegetable kingdom providing varieties of crops, fruits, flowers, medicinal herbs, etc., is not only a rich source of sustenance to man and other living creatures, but also plays an important role in maintaining the ecological balance on earth to the advantage of mankind. The following Verses are worthy of mention in this context:

"And the earth We have spread out

(Like a carpet); set thereon

Mountains firm and immovable;

And produced therein all kinds

Of things in due balance".[45]

"Verily, all things

Have We created

In proportion and measures"[46]

There can be no doubt that the Qur'anic references to plant life inspired the early Muslims to undertake study and research in various fields of botany and agriculture side by side with vigorous cultivation of lands, as a result of which fine botanical and horticultural gardens developed in all parts of the Muslim world for both teaching and experimental purposes. A number of Muslim scientists flourished who devoted themselves to systematic study of plants and their cultivation, and wrote several detailed manuals on the subject which in course of time became the main source material for the development of modern botanical and agricultural sciences. Jabir Ibn Hayyan, Abu Zayd al-Ansari, Ibn-ul-Sikkit, Abu Sa'd al-Asma'i, Abu Hanifah al-Dinawari, al-Ghafiqi and Ibn-ul-

Baytar were noted botanists, while Ibn Wahshiyah, Ibn-ul-'Awwam, etc., were distinguished agricultural scientists.

Of the early Muslim authors who wrote on plant life, Abu Hanifah al-Dinawari (d. 895 C.E.) deserves special mention. His *Kitab-ul-Nabat* on botany in six volumes is massive in size and rich in contents, of which unfortunately only volumes 3 and 6 and fragments of the fourth could be preserved.[47] It covers the classification of plants in general and the morphological structure of the individual plants in three groups-plants cultivated for food, fruit-bearing plants and wild plants.[48] In all he has described 1120 plants. It is an authentic source of information about the medicinal plants also that were known in pre-Islamic Arabia. It is rightly regarded as the first.most comprehensive work on materiae medicae.[49]

It goes to the credit of al-Dinawari that he has thrown sufficient light on sex life of plants in clear terms-the phenomenon which is generally taken to be a recent discovery of modern science. An idea of his sharp observation on this vital aspect of plant life may be derived from the following quotation:

> "Date-palm is so near to animals and even to human beings that sometimes there are love-affairs: sometimes a female date-palm gets amorous of a certain male date-palm. The female tree even physically inclines towards its beloved. If the gardener pollinates this female palm with the pollens of some male palm other than its beloved one, it does not bear fruit, and gets sick until the gardener discovers its beloved tree and "marries them" by sprinkling the pollens of this particular male palm".[50]

In the twelfth century al-Ghafiqi collected a large number of plants from Spain and Africa, and described them accurately. Similarly, Ibn Bajjah was the author of two important books on botony, His *Kitab-ul-Tajribatayn* deals with medicinal herbs, while his *Kitab f-il-Nabat* is devoted to the study of physiology of plants.

Ibn al-Baytar (d. 1249 C.E.), who flourished in Muslim Spain, wrote the most comprehensive book on botany under the title *al-Jami li-Mufradat-il-Adwiyah w-al-Aghdhiyah* which remained the most important encyclopaedia on this subject upto the sixteenth century. It contains detailed descriptions of more then 1400 medicinal plants and herbs, almost four times the number of such plants mentioned by the Greek physician and botanist Diascorides.

The author elaborated for the first time such new concepts as the impact of storage on the nourishing elements of the plants. The information provided by him in this matter played an important role in evolving the scientific methods of storing and preserving medicinal and aromatic plants.

Ibn Wahshiyah (d. 909 C.E.), author of about thirty books, was a renowned agronomist. His most famous work titled *al-Filahah al-Nabatiyah* (The Nabatean Agriculture). covers a variety of subjects on applied agricultural sciences. For example, one chapter is devoted to the discussion of the properties of the olive, while another chapter deals with the science of choosing suitable places for digging wells in order to procure sufficient quantities of water for the purpose of irrigation. The book contains valuable information regarding cultivation of various crops, fruits and vegetables. It also deals with the methods of fighting the diseases and calamities that befall standing crops and plants. It proved so useful and indispensable that it was consulted by almost all the later Muslim authors who wrote on this subject.

Ibn-ul-'Awwam, who flourished in Muslim Spain in the twelfth century, was another important agricultural scientist. His book titled *Kitab al-Filahah* was a significant original contribution to knowledge in the realm of applied agricultural sciences. The author himself studied and described about 585 different plants in addition to the cultivation of more than 50 fruit-bearing trees. The chief merit of the book lies in the fact that it is a storehouse of useful scientific information relating to gardening and agriculture in general.

Divided into 34 sections, the book covers in detail a variety of subjects like species of plants, medicinal and aromatic plants, soil, farming techniques, seasons and methods of plantation of different crops, fruits and vegetables, the science of locating underground water, the techniques of digging wells, irrigation, the methods of preparation and use of different kinds of fertilizers, seed testing technology, plant sex life, etc. He was the first to write on what is known today as the technology of soil. He is also said to have succeeded in making certain trees beer fruits off their season. Similarly, he paid attention to what is known today as seed testing and agricultural industries technology.[51]

Exact and other Sciences

The contributions made by Muslim scholars in exact and other sciences is highly commendable. The names of al-Khwarizmi, the sons of Musa, al-Battani, Ali Bin Yunus, Ibn al-Haytham, al-Biruni, Nasiruddin al-Tusi, al-Qazwini, etc., are very famous for cultivation of exact sciences in Islam. Of them Ali Bin Yunus, Ibn al-Haytham, al-Biruni and al-Tusi deserve special mention in this context.

'Ali Bin Yunus (d. 1009 CE) was the greatest Egyptian astronomer of his time. His principal work is titled as *al-Zij al-Hakimi* (The Hakimi Astronomical Tables) after his patron the Fatimid caliph al-Hakim in which he improved the tables prepared by his predecessors by his original observations and researches. He is also credited with having invented the pendulum for measuring time about six centuries ahead of Galileo, who on his turn studied the subject thoroughly and laid down most of the laws regarding it and its arithmetical implications. It is rightly held by scientists that but for this invention the astronomical science could not have advanced to the position it holds today.[52]

Ibn-ul-Haytham (965-1039 C.E.), popularly known as al-Hazen in the West, was the greatest physicist of his time. His claim to fame rests on his *Kitab-al-Manazir* (The Book of Optics) which, as described by Will Durant, is probably the most thoroughly scientific in its method and thought of all the medieval productions.

Ibn al-Haytham's greatest achievement in the field of optics was that he repudiated the prevalent Greek theory of vision, and presented a correct theory of the process of visual perception, according to which, vision occurs when light emanating from the seen object enters the eye rather than when a ray of light sent by the eye reaches the object as held by Euclid and Ptolemy. He made several other important observations on light which had far-reaching implications in the world of science. For example, prior to his researches, the prevalent view was that light does not take time in reaching from one place to another. It was he who first propounded the theory that light travels at a very fast but fixed speed. But this idea met with severe criticism in intellectual circles until Romer hinted at its possibility towards the end of the 17th century after witnessing two lunar eclipses in succession.[53]

Besides, he anticipated Fermat's principle of Least Time by several centuries by enunciating that a ray of light in passing through a medium takes the easier and quicker path.[54]

Ibn-ul-Haytham also discussed in his *On Twilight Phenomena*, which is now extant only in Latin, the effect of the atmosphere in increasing the apparent size of the sun or the moon near the horizon, and concluded that through atmospheric refraction the light of the sun reaches the earth even when the sun is as much as 19° below the horizon. On this basis he calculated the height of the atmosphere as about 10 English miles.[55]

These and other theories laid down by Ibn-ul-Haytham had a great impact on the advancement of science in the West. This should be clear from the fact that some of his books were translated into the European languages before the Renaissance. Now it is established beyond doubt that such eminent European scientists as Roger Bacon, Witelo, Kepler, Leonardo, etc. were greatly influenced by his researches.[56]

Al-Biruni (973-1050 C.E.) was another eminent scientist and scholar of his time. He was a distinguished astronomer, mathematician, geologist, geographer, pharmacologist, physicist and mineralogist. He contributed a great deal to the development of the Muslim geographical knowledge, especially in the field of mathematical geography. The geographical model of the world and of mankind given by him is accurate to an appreciable extent. He has described the habitable region of the world as follows:

"The plane of the equinoctial cuts the earth at a circle called the equator *(Khatt-ul-Istiwa)* into two parts northern and southern hemispheres. A great circle drawn through the poles divides these two into four quadrants, two northern and two southern. Those who have investigated the matter find that the dry land does not extend beyond one of the northern quadrants. This is therefore called the habitable quadrant. It is as if it were an island surrounded by the sea. In this quarter which men are constantly traversing, they find sees, islands, mountains, rivers and deserts, also towns and villages until towards the north pole a desolate tract is reached of excessive cold, where snows are heaped on snowns".[57]

In addition to the above, al-Biruni made a series of observations on solar transits, lunar eclipses, equinoxes and solstices. He also scientifically described such phenomena as the ebb and flow of tides, earthquakes and even continental shifts.[58] Besides, he propounded his theory of the rotation of the earth on its axis about 600 years ahead of Galileo (1564-1642 C.E.). This is clear from the following passage from his *Canon Masudicus*:

> "When a thing falls from a. height, it does not coincide with the perpendicular line of its descent, but inclines a little, and falls making different angles. When a piece of earth separates from it and falls, it has two kinds of motion: one is the circular motion which it receives from the rotation of the earth, and the other is straight which it acquires in falling directly to the centre of the earth. If it had only the straight motion, it would have fallen to the west of its perpendicular motion. But since both of them exist at one and the same time, it falls neither to the west nor in the perpendicular direction, but a little to the east."[59]

As regards Nasiruddin al-Tusi (1201-1274 C.E.), he made substantial progress in trignometry and planetary astronomy. It was mainly because of his efforts that trignometry achieved the status of an independent branch of pure mathematics. His most original book on this subject is *Kitab Shakl-il-Qatta*, a work on the principle of the transversal, from which he deduced relations of fundamental importance in spherical trignometry.[60] It was translated into Latin, French and English, upon which the Europeans depended for a long time for their knowledge of plane and spherical trignometry. For instance, it was upon this book that Regiomontanus largely depended in the preparation of his own work on trignometry under the title *De Triangulus*.[61]

Another major contribution of Tusi was that he and his colleagues at the magnificent Maraghah Observatory succeeded in getting the close value of precession as 51" (actually 50.26").[62] Further, he considerably advanced the knowledge of planetary astronomy. He produced better planetary models which had a great similarity with those of the Polish astronomer Nicolaus Copernicus. His book *Tadhkirah fi Ilm-il-Hay'ah* contains a survey of the whole field of astronomy. In it he has criticised Ptolemy for his views expressed in *The Almagest*. It was this criticism which enabled Copernicus to enunciate his theory of the celestial bodies which had far-reaching implications for the rise of modern science.[63]

Lastly, the Muslims achieved distinctions in chemistry, oceanography mineralogy, mechanical technology, etc., produced books on them, and made significant contributions to the progress of civilization. It is sufficiently clear from the above brief introduction of this subject that Islam as an educational force not only inspired its followers to promote the cause of knowledge and learning, but also infused in them the spirit of scientific enquiry which is the life and soul of modern sciences. Thus, the Muslims became (during the period of their having been closer to the spirit of Islam) the main bearers of the torch of knowledge and learning as well as harbingers of the modern scientific era. They also religiously cultivated scientific knowledge and shared it with their non-Muslim brethren for the sole constructive purpose of improving the lot of the whole mankind. It is also conclusively established that it is mostly the intellectual foundations of Islam and scientific contributions of the Muslims that present the genuine image of Islam as a mission for the welfare of humanity at large, thereby adequately reflecting the chief ingredients of its dynamism.

References

1. The Qur'an, XXXV: 28.
2. The Qur'an, 11: 31-34.
3. The Qur'an, XCVI : 1-5 (tr. by M. M. Pickthall).
4. The Qur'an, LXVIII: 1-2.
5. For details see Arab-Islamic Legacy to Life Sciences, by Abdul Ali, Delhi, 1993, p. 3.
6. The Qur'an, LIII: 28 (tr. by M. M. Pickthall).
7. The Qur'an, XLIII : 20 (tr. by M. M. Pickthall).
8. Prof. Darwesh Mustafa *"Tarikh al-Umam fi al-Hadarat al-Islamiyah"* in the Journal *Manar al-Islam*, January-1977, p. 87.
9. Prof. Abdus Salam : "Islam and Science" in *Hamdard Medicus*, Pakistan, Vol. XXIX, No. 4, p. 3.
10. The Qur'an, L: 7-8 (tr. by Yusuf Ali).
11. The Qur'an, LXXXVIII: 17-20.
12. The Qur'an, VII: 179.

13. The Qur'an, XXXV: 12 (tr. by M. M. Pickthall).
14. The Qur'an, XXI: 33 (tr. by M.M. Pickthall).
15. The Qur'an, XV: 22 (tr. by M.M. Pickthall).
16. The Qur'an, XXIV: 43.
17. M. M. Pickthall, *Cultural Side of Islam*, p. 68.
18. The Qur'an, XXXVI : 35.
19. The Qur'an, LXXV: 36-40.
20. The Qur'an, LXXV: 43 (tr. by M. M. Pickthall).
21. Ibrahim Bin Syed : "The Qur'anic Comets of Ice" in *The Muslim World League Journal*, Saudi Arabia, Vol. XVI, Nos. 1 & 2, pp. 10-11.
22. Prof. Abdus Salam, *op. cit.*, p 4.
23. Maurice Bucaille, *The Bible, the Qur'an and Science*, p. vii.
24. Mukarram Muhammad Ahmad in the Journal *Al-Arabi*, Kuwait, No. 221, p. 32.
25. 'Umar al-Dasuqi, *Fi al-Adab al-Hadith*, Cairo, Vol. I, p. 474.
26. For details see *Arab-Islamic Legacy to Life Sciences, op. cit.*, pp. 12-32.
27. Dr. Ahmad Shawqi al-Fanjari : "*Al-Tibb al-Wiqa-i-f-il-Islam*" in the Journal *Al-'Arabi*, Kuwait, No. 202, pp. 56-57.
28. G. Bernard Shaw, *The Doctor's Dilemma*, ed. by A.C. Ward, p. 80.
29. *Encyclopaedia Britannica*, Vol. XV, p. 203.
30. P. K. Hitti, *History of the Arabs*, p. 577.

31. Dr. Ali Mubarak : "*Alaman Arabiyan fi Sama-il-Tibb*" in the Journal *Al-'Arabi*, Kuwait, No. 354, May, 1988, p. 67.

32. *The Macimillan Everyman's Encyclopaedia*, Fourth Edition, New York, 1959, Vol. III, p. 265.

33. *The Genius of Arab Civilization*, ed. by John R. Hayes, 1983, p. 182.

34. The Qur'an, XXII: 5 (tr. by Yusuf Ali).

35. *The Times of India*, New Delhi, December 10, 1984, p. 9.

36. The Qur'an, II : 259 (tr. by Yusuf Ali).

37. P. K. Hitti, *History of the Arabs*, p. 382.

38. Mehmet Bayrakdar: "Al-Jahiz and the Rise of Biological Evolutionism", in *Hamdard Islamicus*, Vol. VIII, No. 2, 1985, p. 34.

39. *Ibid.*, p. 34.

40. *Ibid.*, p. 36.

41. *The Genius of Arab Civilization, op. cit.*, p. 183.

42. Muhammad Hamidullah: "Early Muslim Contribution to Botany" in the Journal *Al-'Ilm*, Vol. V (January 1985), p. 5.

43. The Qur'an, XXI: 30.

44. Maurice Bucaille, *The Bible, the Qur'an and Science*, p. 186.

45. The Qur'an, XV: 19 (tr. by Yusuf Ali).

46. LIV: 49, *Ibid.*

47. Muhammad Hamidullah, *op. cit.*, p. 9.

48. E. J. Brill, *First Encyclopaedia of Islam*, Vol. II, p. 978.

49. Hakim Muhammad Said : "Islamic Medicine and the Art of Drug-Making—a Historical Perspective" in *Hamdard Medicus*, Vol. XXXIII, No. 1, 1990, p. 47.
50. Muhammad Hamidullah, *op. cit.*, p. 9.
51. For details see *Arab-Islamic Legacy to Life Sciences* by Abdul Ali, Delhi, 1993, pp. 88-98.
52. Umar A. Farrukh, 1954, *The Arab Genius in Science and Philosophy*, tr. from Arabic by John B. Hardie, pp. 67-68, Washington.
53. N. Shahin, 1976 "*Hasan Bin at-Haytham, Qafilat al-Zayt*" (August), p. 38, Saudi Arabia.
54. Prof. Abdus Salem "Islam and Science" *Hamdard Medicus*, Vol. XX IX, No. 4: p. 5, Pakistan.
55. Will Durant, *The Story of Civilization*, Vol. IV, p. 288.
56. *Ibid.*, p. 289.
57. Ibrahim Boolaki: "The Mathematical Geography of al-Biruni" in *Hamdard Islamicus*, Pakistan, Vol. VII, No. 2, 1984, pp. 64-65.
58. *Ibid.*, p. 66.
59. *A History of Muslim Philosophy*, ed. by M. M. Shareef, 1989, Vol. II, p. 1290.
60. E. J. Brill, *First Encyclopaedia of Islam*, Vol. VIII, p. 981.
61. Qadri Hafiz Tuqan, *Al-'Ulum 'ind al-Arab*, p. 210.
62. Seyyed Houssein Nasr in *Dictionary of Scientific Biography*, New York, Vol, XIII, p. 509.
63. Dr. Abdul Azim Anis : "*Nasir al-Din al-Tusi*" in the Journal *Al-'Arabi*, Kuwait, 330 (May 1986), pp. 37-39.

9

Arab-Islamic Legacy to Humour Literature

Humour has been one of the most potent instruments of all time. Down the ages, clowns and comedians have entertained the masses as well as provided them with the best medicine in the form of laughter which is known to serve as a safety valve for the release of pent up tensions and emotions. It was chiefly for this reason that they even enjoyed the licence to speak the unspeakable with an eye on causing laughter among their listeners.

In modern times psychiatrists and physicians have also highlighted the therapeutic value of laughter by describing it as one of the best stress-busters. As held by them, it has a healthy effect "on almost all the major systems of the human body: autonomous nervous system, circulatory system, respiratory system, skeletal muscular system, central nervous system, the immune and endocrine system".[1] It is also known to stimulate the heart and the brain.

Like all other peoples of the world, the Arabs also possess a rich legacy of humour literature. But this fact is hardly known outside the Arab world. On the contrary, the impression which the average educated non-Arab reader has about them is that they are totally deprived of the faculty of humour. The Arabs of the medieval times, the period of their intellectual and cultural ascendancy, are generally portrayed by Muslim historians as having been serious cultivators of knowledge and learning as well as 'fighters during the day and worshippers during the night'. It is surprising to note that in their historical accounts of this people they have failed to give even a passing reference to their lighter side which has remained a striking feature of their cultural and social life not only in the pre-Islamic period, but also in the Islamic times.

It would be no exaggeration to say that a true picture of the Arab life and nature is not possible without taking into account the lighter side of this people, who had a highly cultivated sense of humour with a remarkable capacity for cracking jokes. This is clearly borne out by the fact that Arabic literature abounds in jokes, light talks and humorous anecdotes. Volumes upon volumes of classical Arabic literature are devoted wholly to humour, which unfortunately have not yet received adequate attention of modern scholars. Perhaps, the main reason for this is that humour is not easily translatable. Hence, an attempt is made below to give an account of the lighter side of the Arabs in the light of the Islamic sanction for humour.

Islamic Sanction for Humour

It is remarkable to note that even the pre-Islamic Arabs, who spent most of their days in inter-tribal hostilities, were found to be a jolly and sociable lot. They also exchanged anecdotes and recited poetry at the social and cultural gatherings which they occasionally held during the four sacred months—*i.e., Dhul-Qa'dah, Dhul-Hijjah, Muharram* and *Rajab*—

in which war was prohibited among them. Indeed, it is a matter of great credit for them that they almost fully observed the sanctity of these months despite the fact that there was no central government to enforce it. Thus, called upon to lead a hard life, they seemed fully acquainted with the value of laughter in line with what was later nicely described by the modern thinker F. Moore Colby in the sentence: "Total absence of humour renders life impossible".[2] Their liking for humour is further evidenced by the fact that they named their sons and daughters as *Dahhak* (great laughter), *Bassam* (smiling), *Jadhlan* (cheerful), *Talq* or *Taliq* (having a bright face), *Bashir* (messenger of happy news), *Bishr* (joyful countenance), *Maymunah* (auspicious lady), *Masudah* (lucky lady), etc. This point is further elaborated by the fact that when the Arabs praised anyone, they described him to be a person who would heartily laugh as well as become cheerful at the arrival of guests at his house. But when they blamed anyone, they presented him to be a grim-faced, peevish person of hateful appearance as if his face was sprinkled with vinegar, and mustard oil was applied into his nose.[3]

Later, the religion of Islam as preached by Prophet Muhammad (P.B.H.), contrary to popular perception, never aimed at stifling the instinct of sound humour in man. It rather sharpened and made it sophisticated. This is clearly borne out by the following Apostolic traditions as well as statements of the Prophet's Companions and other religious authorities.

> Prophet Muhammad (P.B.H.) is reported to have said:
>
> Cheer up the hearts from time to time. Otherwise, if the hearts get tired, they would be rendered blind.[4]
>
> There is no worth in the person who neither rejoices, nor makes others rejoice.

Nu'ayman entered Paradise laughing, because he used to make me laugh.'

Once the Prophet (P.B.H.) visited Nu'ayman, one of whose eyes was afflicted with ophthalmia. On seeing him eat date, the Prophet (P.B.H.) said: "Although you are suffering from ophthalmia, yet you are eating date". He replied: "Yes, but I am eating it from the other eye". On hearing this the Prophet (P.B.H.) laughed so heartily that his molar teeth appeared.[7]

Again, a small slave-girl of a certain Ansar used to visit the Prophet's wife, Hadrat 'Aishah (R.U.) frequently and make her laugh by playing in her presence. Sometimes, the Prophet (P.B.H.) also happened to be there, and both laughed together. But once when the Prophet (P.B.H.) missed her for a long period, he enquired from Hadrat 'Aishah (R.U.) about her. When she informed him that she was ill, he went to her house and found her on her death-bed. He asked the members of her house to inform him in case she died. When she died, the Prophet (P.B.H.) himself led her funeral prayer, and prayed to Allah to make her laugh heartily as she used to make them laugh.[8]

In the light of the above and similar Apostolic traditions it may fairly be claimed for the Prophet (P.B.H.) that he never gave any trace of narrow-mindedness or rigidity in his private as well as public lifestyle. He was found full of pleasant and delightful humour. As reported by Anas, he mixed up with his Companions on familiar terms as well as joked and laughed with them. Once the Prophet (P.B.H.) addressed this reporter when the latter was inattentive in a lighter vein, saying: "O you with the two ears!", thereby meaning very obedient.[9] It is also related that an old lady once visited the Prophet (P.B.H.) and asked him to pray for her so that she might enter Paradise. He replied jokingly: "No old woman will enter

Paradise". Being grieved at this answer, she began crying. Then the Prophet (P.B.H.) asked his Companions to tell her that she would enter Paradise as a young girl.[10]

Further, the Prophet (P.B.H.) maintained his elasticity, saying: "Indeed, I have been sent with the accommodating straightforward religion".[11] As such he was not against laughter-provoking humour, provided it did not exceed the bounds of decency and moderation. He is on record as having said: "I do joke, but I always speak the truth".[12] At the same time he was not in favour of excess of humour and laughter, because, as described by him, "too much of laughter kills the heart".[13]

Following sayings and anecdotes of the Companions of the Prophet (P.B.H.) and scholars emphasize the importance of humour:

'Ali bin Abi Talib[14]

Cheer up the hearts and entertain them with the anecdotes of wisdom. Otherwise, they will become tired like the body.[15]

Whosoever has the element of witticism in him, he is cured of vanity and haughtiness.[16]

Usamah bin Zayd[17]

Entertain the hearts; and they will worship Allah.[18]

Abu al-Darda'[19]

Entertain the soul with a little of *batil* (light talk) in order to get its cooperation in the cause of truth.[20]

'Amr Ibn al-As[21]

Once it was said to him: "What is the most delicious thing to you?" He replied after bidding the minors leave the room: "The most delicious thing to me is putting off the garb of manliness".[22]

Muhammad Bin Muslim al-Zuhri[23]

The ears and the hearts also do get fed up (with too much of religious and academic discussion). So let me listen to your poems and light conversations.[24]

'Umar Bin 'Abd al-'Aziz[25]

When one day the caliph was reminded by his son 'Abd al-Malik to attend to the needs of the people who had assembled at his door rather than to continue sleeping in the forenoon he said: "My dear son! My soul is my riding-beast. If I emaciate it, I would exaust it. And whosoever exhausts the riding-beast, he cannot reach his destination".[26]

Hisham Bin 'Abd al-Malik[27]

I do not find anything more delicious for me than a friend, between whom and me there does not exist the barrier of reservation.[28]

Ibn 'Abd Rabbih[29]

Witticism is the entertainment of the soul, spring of the heart, pasturage of the ear and a great source of comfort and happiness.[30]

Abu Hayyan al-Tawhidi[31]

Refrain from refusing to listen to jokes and humorous anecdotes. If you forsake them altogether, your power of perception will certainly weaken, while your temper will show signs of stupidity. And nothing sharpens the intellect more than examining the affairs of the world and acquiring knowledge of its good and bad things as well as its known and secret matters. So make your familiarity with jokes a means of entertaining yourself and your enjoyment with them a ladder to your seriousness. Otherwise, if you don't let yourself taste the pleasure of humour, the grief of seriousness will distress you.[32]

It is clear from the above that far from considering humour a taboo, even the greatest religious authorities of Islam including Prophet Muhammad (P.B.H.) highlighted the importance of laughter-provoking humour in the life of man. It would be no exaggeration to say that they were fully acquainted not only with the therapeutic value of laughter, but also with the numerous other advantages of leading a jolly and cheerful life, in the realization of which humour has an important role to play. It is important to note in this context that the Islamic approach to humour is further substantiated by the following Qur'anic verses in which assuming a stern and gloomy countenance has been disapproved, while merriment and cheerfulness have been described as among the characteristic features of life in Paradise:

Then he (the disbelieving one) frowned and scowled. (Al-Qur'an, LXXIV:22)

The Prophet frowned and turned away, because there came to him the blind man. (Al-Qur'an, LXXX:1-2)

Verily, the Companions of the Garden shall that day have joy. (Al-Qur'an, XXXVI:55)

As to the Righteous, they will be in Gardens, and in happpiness, enjoying the Bliss which their Lord hath bestowed on them. (Al-Qur'an, LII:17-18)

Main Features of Arab-Muslim Humour Literature

The most characteristic feature of Arab jokes and humorous anecdotes is that they were not the product of the imagination of their professional comedians living in isolation from society, but they arose out of everyday situations. Thus, they are such as have actually occured in the practical life. Even their professional humorists, who remained wholly devoted to making jokes and sponging on others, interacted with the people, and made their witty remarks on the stage of real life rather than in their private hours. The Arab jokes, therefore, not only entertain the reader, but also provide him with penetrating insights into the main trends of life that prevailed in the Arab-Muslim societies in those days.

The next important feature of the Arab jokes is that they are sometimes quite earthly, sometimes highly sublime. At the same time there is no dearth of vile and obscene or non-vegetarian jokes also which have been duly recorded even by renowned and revered Arab authors. Some of them are so vulgar that they should better be included only in a pornographic work. For instance, the book *al-Imta' wa'l-Mu'anasah* comprising three volumes by Abu Hayyan al-Tawhidi is a storehouse of both sound and vulgar jokes. Dr. Ahmad Amin, who edited this work, was fully aware of this fact which he has expressed, saying: "But for intellectual honesty, I would have dropped most of them".[33]

Main Arab Authors on Humour Literature

The importance which the Arabs gave to the role of humour in life is further substantiated by the large number of voluminous books produced by them on this subject. Some important such books are: *al-Bukhala* (The Misers) by al-Jahiz (d. 868-9 C.E.); the *'Uyun al-Akhbar* (Fountains of Information) by Ibn Qutaybah (d. 889 C.E.); *al-'Iqd al-Farid* (The Unique Necklace) by Ibn 'Abd Rabbih (860-940 C.E.); the *Kitab al-Diyarat* (The Book of Monasteries) by Abu al-Hasan 'Ali bin Muhammad al-Shabushti (d. 1008 C.E.); *al-Imta' wal-Mu'anasah* (Enjoyment and Sociability) and *al-Basa'ir wa'l-Dhakha'ir* (Clear Sights and Treasures) by Abu Hayyan al-Tawhidi (d. 1010 C.E.); *Jam 'al-Jawahir fi'l-Mulah wa'l-Nawadir* (Collection of Gems on Witticisms and Humorous Anecdotes) by Abu Ishaq Ibrahim al-Husri al-Qayrawani (d. 1061 C.E.); *al-Tatfil wa Hakayat al-Tufayliyin* (Sponging and the Tales of Spongers) by al-Khatib al-Baghdadi (d. 1071 C.E.), etc. All these works contain rich treasures of Arabic humour literature.

In addition to the above, large numbers of jokes and witticisms are also found in the works of such pious and religious Arab authors as 'Abd al-Malik bin Muhammad al-Tha'alibi (961-1038 C.E.), author of the *Yatimat al-Dahr fi Mahasin Ahl il-'Asr* (The Unique Pearl of the Time on the Merits of the Contemporary People); Abu al-Qasim al-Husayn al-Isfahani (d. 1108 C.E.), author of the *Muhadarat al-Udaba* (Lectures of the Men of Letters) and *al-Mufradat fi Gharib il-Qur'an* (Strange Words of the Qur'an); Yaqut al-Hamawi (1179-1229 C.E.), author of the *Mujam al-Buldan* (The Dictionary of Countries) and the *Mujam al-Udaba* (The Dictionary of Litterateurs); Ibn Khallikan (1211-1282 C.E.), author of the *Wafayat al-Ayan wa Anba Abnail-Zaman* (Obituaries of Prominent Men and Biographies of Eminent Contemporaries); Shihab al-Din Ahmad al-Nuwayri (d. 1332 C.E.), author of the *Nihayat al-Arab fi Funun il-Adab* (The Extreme End on the Branches of Literature); Ibn Fadlillah al-'Umari (1301-1349 C.E.), author of the *Masalik al-Absar* (The Paths of Sights), etc. It is remarkable to note that even these authors did not see any fault in including a good number of humorous anecdotes in their works that were principally devoted to the discussion of serious matters.

Sources and Specimens of Arab Humour

Like all other peoples the Arabs too had their folk humorists as well as professional comedians. Their main folk humorist Juha, perhaps a mythical figure, was represented by them as an ordinary family man, in whose words several humorous anecdotes and witty remarks were narrated by them. Consider, for example, the following:

> One day Juha purchased a bag of flour, and hired a porter to carry it. On the way the porter dodged

> him and went away with the bag. A few days later, when Juha saw him, he hid himself from the latter. When he was asked about it, he said: "I fear that he may demand from me his wages for carrying the bag".[34]

> Some persons saw Juha run in the market one day. When they asked him why he was running, he enquired whether a slave-girl belonging to a man sporting dyed beard passed by them.[35]

One day Juha went to a public bath. But the attendants of the bath gave him old, dirty towels; and they did not pay him the attention which he deserved. Nevertheless, be put the big amount of 10 *qurush* (singular of *qirsh,* a Turkish denomination of currency) near the mirror at the time of his departure from them. The attendants were but naturally much pleased to receive the unexpected amount. Juha visited the bath again after a week. Now the attendants paid him extraordinary respect and attention. They also gave him clean embroidered towels and silken waistwrappers. Meanwhile, Juha observed all that silently without saying anything. But when at the time of his departure, he put only one qirsh near the mirror, the attendants wondered as well as became angry with him at his payment of the paltry amount. Then Juha said: "There is nothing unusual in it. The payment which I have made today is meant for the previous visit; and the previous payment was meant for this visit".[36]

> One day Juha tried to enkindle fire in the oven, but he could not succeed. Then he put the scarf of his wife on his head, and started blowing again into the oven, which now caught fire. Seeing this, he exclaimed: "Wonderful! Even the oven is afraid of my wife".[37]

> Once a certain rich man said to Juha: "If you spit on the face of one of my enemies, I will pay you a handsome amount of money". Juha agreed to do this work. He went to the said man and spat on his face. The man became angry with Juha and took him to the court of law. When the judge asked Juha about it, he said: "Yes, I have done it, and I am authorised by a decree to that effect". Greatly surprised at this statement, the judge asked Juha to show him the decree. Then Juha handed over to the judge a purse containing half the amount of money which he had received from his rich friend. As soon as the judge looked into the purse, he turned his face towards the complainant, saying: "Truly, your opponent has shown me a decree which confers upon him the right to spit on your face as well as on the faces of all the people including myself".[38]

As regards the professional Arab humorists, Ash'ab, Abu Nuwas, Muzayyid, Abu al-'Ayna', to name only a few, were particularly very famous. They were not only sharp-minded and well-informed, but also capable of cracking jokes on all possible subjects. Some of the witty remarks made by them are translated below.

Ash'ab

> One day Ash'ab borrowed a large bowl from his neighbours. He returned it the next day to the owners along with a smaller bowl, saying that the large bowl had given birth to the smaller one. Some time later, he borrowed the large bowl again, and retained it with him. When the owners enquired about it, he told them that it had died in labour. "How can a bowl die in labour?", they asked. "If it can give birth, why can't it die in labour?" was his instant reply.[40]

Once Ash'ab completed his prayer in a very short time. Someone in the mosque pointed it out to him, saying: "Ash'ab, you have finished your prayer very quickly". He replied: "Yes, it was an unadultrated prayer which did not have any trace of hypocrisy".[41]

Once Ash'ab's beloved asked him to give her a ring, saying that she would remember him by it. He said: "Remember me this way that you asked me for something, but I did not give it to you".[42]

One day Salim Bin 'Abd Allah, the governor of Madinah, went out picnicking to the outskirts of the city along with his family members. When Ash'ab, came to know about it, he also left for that place with an eye on sponging on him. Finding the door closed upon his reaching there, he intruded upon them by scaling the wall. Then Salim rebuked him, saying: "Woe to you 0 Ash'ab! Don't you see that I am here along with my wife and daughters?" In reply Ash'ab suggestively recited the Qur'anic verse embodying the answer of the disbelieving sodomists from amongst the people of prophet Lot (A.S.) when the latter offered them his own daughters in order to keep them away from the good-looking Divine guests he had just received: "Well you know that we have no claim to your daughters, and well you know what we want".[43] Then Salim laughed, and offered Ash'ab sufficient quantity of food which he ate as well as carried to his house.[44]

It was said to Ash'ab: "Had you memorized the Apostolic traditions (Sayings of Prophet Muhammad [P.B.H.]) as you have done the jokes, it would have been much better for you". He said: "I have done it". Then they asked him to relate a Tradition. He said: "As narrated to me by Nafi' on the authority of Ibn Umar,'[45] the Prophet (P.B.H.) said: Whosoever has the two traits in him, he is recorded as a sincere friend of Allah". They said: "This is a fine Tradition indeed. What are these two traits?". Ash'ab jokingly replied: "My narrator Nafi' forgot one and I forgot the other".[46]

One day Ash'ab was eating dates along with Salim. When the latter saw him eat two dates together, he said: "Ash'ab, the Messenger of Allah has prohibited the eating of two dates together". Then Ash'ab replied, saying: "Be silent. By Allah, if the Prophet (P.B.H.) had seen such inferior quality of dates, he would have certainly permitted to eat a handful of it together".[47]

Abu Nuwas[48]

While Abu Nuwas was sitting in the company of some eminent men of letters in a tavern owned by a merchant of Baghdad, there came to him a man and said: "O Abu Nuwas, I am feeling such a severe pain in my belly as if my intestines are going to be torn to pieces". Abu Nuwas looked at him and said: "What did you eat yesterday evening?" The man said: "To tell you the truth, I ate only one round cake of barley". Abu Nuwas replied: "Then you should better consult a veterinarian, for he is more competent to treat you than I myself". The man felt greatly ashamed, and went away.[49]

It is said that one day Abu Nuwas visited a friend, who was very miserly; and at that time he was having fever. The physician also visited and examined him and said: "This patient will not be cured of this fever unless he sweats severely". Then Abu Nuwas said: "If you people want him to sweat immediatley, you should eat in his presence of the food of his house, for that will cause him to sweat severely, and thus he will be cured of this fever". Then all those present in the house burst into laughter.[50]

When Abu Nuwas fell ill, his friend al-Jammaz visited him and said: "Fear Allah, for you have censured so many chaste ladies and committed so many sins. So, now you should repent of your misdeeds before death overtakes you". Abu Nuwas said: "You have spoken the truth, but I am not going to repent". When al-Jammaz enquired about the reason, Abu Nuwas retorted: "For fear that its credit will go to a wicked man like you".[51]

Muzayyid[52]

Muzayyid said: "If anyone in the past fell in love with a girl, first he corresponded with her for a year, and then he agreed to chew the raisin which she chewed. After that when they met, they conversed and recited poetry. But today if anyone falls in love with a girl, be straight away wants to cohabit with her with the authority as if his *nikah* (marriage) with her was witnessed by Abu Hurayrah" (a renowned narrator of Apostolic Traditions).[53]

Abu Habib used to make Caliph Mahdi laugh by memorizing and relating to him the witticisms of Muzayyid, for which he was duly rewarded, whereupon the latter said to the former: "May my father be your ransom! I am sowing, while you are reaping".[54]

Once Muzayyid clothed his wife a shirt made of rough cloth. When she complained to him of the roughness of the cloth, he silenced her, saying:."Do you find it more rough than divorce?[55]

Abu al-Ayna'[56]

Once Abu al-'Ayna' entered upon (attended) Caliph al-Mutawakkil in the latter's prestigious Jafari palace. The caliph said to him "Tell me your impression of this palace of ours". Abu al-Ayn-a' said: "People build houses in the world, but you have built the world in your house". And the caliph was greatly impressed by this statement.[57]

A certain minister once made Abu al-'Ayna' ride a beast of burden, and then he waited for its fodder to be brought. But when he thus detained Abu al-'Ayna' long, the latter said: "O minister! You have mounted me upon the beast or the beast upon me".[58]

When a certain Said was appointed as minister following his conversion to Islam, Abu-al-'Ayna visited his house; but it was said to him that the minister was busy offering prayers. And when on his second visit it was again said to him that the minister was engaged in prayers, he commented: "He is excused, because every new thing has its own pleasure".[59]

When Abu al-'Ayna' visited 'Ubayd Allah bin Sulayman holding a high post, the latter refused to meet him saying that he was very busy. Then Abu al-'Ayna' retorted: "And when you become free, *i.e.*, discharged from office, I cease to be in need of you".[60]

Besides, there were several other categories of people, who provided Arabic literature with rich humour. The misers were one such prominent community, about whom the Arabs never tired of telling tales. The renowned Arab belletrist al-Jahiz has written a masterpiece on them under the title *al-Bukhala*, which is not only full of humour, but also contains lively insights into the behaviour and psychology of misers. The anecdotes translated below are intended to give the reader an idea of this variety of Arab humour.

While a certain governor of Persia was busy in his office, there appeared before him a poet, who sang an ode, in which he highly praised and glorified the dignitary. When he finished his panegyric, the governor appreciated him and ordered his accountant to pay him 10,000 *dirhams* as a reward. The poet became so happy at the sanction of the reward that he was totally astounded. When the governor saw his verbal order having such a great impact upon the poet, he increased the amount of the reward to 20,000 *dirhams*. Now the happiness of the poet knew no bounds. Seeing that the happiness of the poet was increasing manifold in proportion to the verbal increase in the amount of the reward, he raised the amount to 40,000 *dirhams*. Now the poet was about to die of happiness. Then the accountant said to the governor: "Glory be to Allah! The poet would have become fully satisfied with only 40 *dirhams*. Why did you order payment of 40,000 *dirhams* to him?" 'Woe to you! Do you want to give him something?", asked the governor. When the accountant said that he was bound to implement his order, the latter replied: "O fool! This man has pleased us only with his speech. So, we have also pleased him with our speech. And when he described me to be more beautiful than the moon, more powerful than the lion, more sharp-tongued than the sword and more effective than the spear-head, be did not give me anything which I could carry home. Don't we know that he has only told a lie? But while telling a lie, he has pleased us. Thus, we have also pleased him by issuing false verbal orders for payment of rewards to him. In this way there will be speech for speech and falsehood for falsehood. Otherwise, if truth is returned for falsehood and reward for speech, this will be a sheer loss".[61]

One day a banquet was given by al-Mughirah bin Abu 'Abd Allah al-Thaqfi, the governor of Kufa. A roasted kid was served on his dining table which neither the governor himself, nor anyone else touched. In the meantime a bedouin attended the feast, and started eating and devouring the meat of the kid in rather an uncivilized manner. Wanting to shame him, the governor said: "I see that you are eating the kid with such fierceness as if its mother had once butted you with its horns". Then the bedouin retorted: "May Allah keep you fit, and I see that you are pitying it as if its mother had breastfed you".[62]

A certain miser said to his slave: "Bring the meal and close the door". The slave replied: "My lord, what you have said is decidedly wrong. You should have rather ordered me first to close the door and then to bring you the meal". This statement of the slave appealed to his miserly master so much that he set him free forthwith, saying: "Now you are free for the sake of Allah for the sound wisdom displayed by you in this matter."[63]

Someone once said to Thumamah bin Ashras: "I want you to do me a work". Thumamah said: "I also want you to do me a work". The man said: "And what is the work which you want me to do for you?" Thumamah said: "I won't tell it to you unless you promise to do it". When the man promised to get his work done, the latter said: "My work is that you should not ask me to do any work for you". Then the man departed from him, disappointed.[64]

The numerous false prophets, who appeared at close intervals throughout the Islamic centuries, were also known to raise a good laugh by their presence of mind and witty remarks:

Someone claimed to be a prophet in the time of Caliph al-Mahdi. He was captured and produced before the caliph. When the caliph asked him whether he was a prophet, be replied in the affirmative. When the caliph further asked him to whom he was sent, he said angrily: "You did not give me a chance to go to any people. I received my mission in the morning and you got me arrested and imprisoned in the evening". This evoked laughter of the caliph, who presented him some amount of money, and set him free, saying: "You are true, we have acted hastily in your case!".[65]

Some one claimed prophethood in the time of Caliph al-Ma'mun. When he was captured and brought before the Caliph, the latter said: "What is the proof of your prophethood ?" He said: "The proof is that I can tell you what you are hiding in your heart". When the caliph asked him to tell it, he replied: "May Allah keep you fit, at present you are thinking that I am a liar". On hearing this, the caliph laughed at him and set him free.[66]

Someone claimed to be a prophet in the time of Caliph al-Mamun. When he was asked about his miracle, he said: "I will throw before you a pebble in water, and it will get dissolved in it". When he was asked to do so, he took out a pebble which he had kept with him, and threw it into water which got dissolved in it. The caliph said: "This is an act of deceit. You should dissolve in water a pebble given by us". The false prophet said: "Neither you are mightier than Pharaoh, nor am I greater than Moses. Even Pharaoh never asked prophet Moses to perform his miracle of turning into a serpent a staff given by the former, rather than his own staff'. The caliph laughed and gave him a reward.[67]

Once a certain woman claiming prophethood for herself was produced before Caliph al-Mamun, who interrogated her as follows:

Caliph	:	"Who are you?"
Woman	:	"I am Fatimah, the prophetess".
Caliph	:	"Do you have faith in the religion preached by Prophet Muhammad (P.B.H.)?"
Woman	:	"Everything taught and preached by Muhammad (P.B.H.) is true".

Caliph : "But the Prophet (P.B.H.) said that there would be no more prophets after him".

Woman : "The Prophet (P.B.H.) has rightly said so, but he never said that there would be no prophetess after me".

On hearing this, the caliph burst into laughter and covered his face.[68]

Next, simpletons and stupid persons from all sections of society were also a rich source of humour in Arabic, who used to make people laugh by their foolish acts and behaviour:

> Muhammad bin Ahmad al-Tirmidhi, a distinguished Shafiite jurist, said: "Once I was sitting with-al-Zajjaj along with a host of eminent men and scholars who had assembled to offer their condolences to him on the death of his mother. In the meantime Ibn al-Jassas entered the room laughing and said: "Praise be to Allah, O Zajjaj! I am much pleased to hear the news". Al-Zajjaj and all those present were greatly astonished to hear him say like this. It was said to him: "Poor fellow! How can that please you which has greatly grieved him and us". He replied boldly and confidently: "Woe to thee! Originally, the news reached me that al-Zajjaj himself has died, but when it became clear to me that she has died, I became happy". Then all the people assembled there laughed at him.[69]

A certain dupe once visited a sick person. While departing from him, he turned towards his family members and said: "This time don't repeat what you did in case of such a one who died, but you did not inform us. So if this one dies, please do inform us, so that we may participate in his funeral prayer."[70]

An aged woman visited a family to offer her condolences on the death of one of its members. While she was departing from them, she saw a sick person in the house. Then she turned back and said to them: "By Allah, it is difficult for me to walk. So, I offer you my condolences in advance in case of this sick person also".[71]

Once a slave-girl complained to her master Abu Damdam against a particular person, saying: "He has kissed me". The master said: "You kiss him too, for Allah has prescribed retaliation for wounds".[72]

A certain person once promised one of his brothers to present him a mule. But when he delayed fulfillment of his promise, the brother took a small bottle, stored in it his urine, and brought it to his physician, saying: "Doctor, look into this water and tell me whether my brother will present me a mule".[73]

Another important category of people who provided Arabic literature with rich humour was that of spongers who used to attend feasts as uninvited quests. They also evoked laughter of the people by the tricks and deceits used by them in their attempts at intruding at matrimonial feasts:

Muhammad bin Sa'id once said to a sponger: "Woe to you! You are eating prohibited food". The sponger said: I always eat lawful food". When Muhammad asked him to justify his sponging, he said: "Whenever I enter a house on the occasion of a feast, I straightaway go to the door meant for ladies. On seeing me do that people invariably start calling me 'come here, come here', and their calling me 'come here' amounts to an invitation. Thus, I eat only lawful food".[74]

When a sponger visited a matrimonial feast, he was not allowed entry into it. But he knew that one of the brothers of the bride was out of station, and that he could not attend the function. So he took a piece of paper, and folded and sealed it without putting anything into it. Then he wrote on it the address (from the brother to the bride), visited the feast again, and said to the organizers that he was carrying a letter addressed to the bride from her brother. When they permitted him to enter the house, he entered and handed the letter over to the bride. When they saw the envelope, they said: "We have never seen such address beforehand, for the name of none is written on it". And the sponger added to their wonder, saying" "What is more surprising than this is the fact that there is nothing, not even a single word inside the envelope, for the brother was in great haste". Then they came to know that he was a sponger, who resorted to that strategem to intrude at the feast. They also laughed at him as well as fed him.[75]

There passed a sponger by people who were having their lunch. The sponger said: "*Assalam 'Alaykum*, O wicked people!". They objected, saying: "No, by Allah, we are noble people". Then he bent his legs and sat down, praying: "O Allah! Make their statement true and my statement false".[76]

Once a certain sponger saw a group of heretics being taken to a place to be sentenced to death. Seeing their good appearance and clean dresses, he presumed that they were invited to a feast. So he gently joined their group and became one of them. When he appeared before the police officer on his turn, he said: "May Allah keep you fit, I am not one of the heretics. I am only a sponger. I joined their group only when I presumed that they were being taken to a feast". The police officer said: "This tactic is not going to save you from me". And he ordered his men to behead him. Then the sponger said: "May Allah keep you fit, if you have finally decided to kill me, please order the executioner to strike my belly with the sword, because it is only the belly which has put me into this dilemma". Then the police officer laughed and enquired about him. And when he came to know that the man was a known sponger, he set him free.[77]

Besides, large numbers of humorous anecdotes and witty remarks were minted at the tongues of various other categories of people, especially caliphs, bedouins, grammarians, slave-girls, beggars, etc. Some such anecdotes are translated below to give the reader an idea of the richness of these sources of Arab humour:

When Abu al-Janadi divorced his wife, she said: "'Is this the reward of having lived with you for fifty years?" The husband replied: "And you are charged with no other crime".[78]

Once a certain man was found in possession of a vessel of wine. He was arrested and produced before the magistrate of his town. On seeing the tool of wine with him, the magistrate sentenced him to the penalty for drinking wine. When the man asked the magistrate about the cause of the punishment, the latter told him that his crime was established on the basis of his being in possession of the tool of wine. The man said: "Then you should sentence me to the penalty for fornication also". When the magistrate asked him about the cause of it, the latter replied: "Because I am possessing the tool of fornication also". On hearing this argument, the magistrate burst into laughter, and set the accused free.[79]

When the people of Kufa complained to Caliph al-Ma'mun against their governor, the caliph defended the governor by saying that he was the most just and upright of all his governors. They said: "O Amir al-Mu'minin ! If such is the merit of this governor, then let all the provinces have a share in him, so that they all may get an equal measure of justice; and if the caliph does that, he cannot remain governor over us for more than three months". On hearing this argument, the caliph laughed and dismissed the governor from office.[80]

Somebody once hired from a learned man a house, the old wooden ceiling of which was causing lot of cracking sound. When the owner of the house visited the tenant for the rent, the latter requested him to repair the ceiling as it was causing much cracking sound. "Don't worry, it is only glorifying the name of Allah", said the owner. "But my worry is that Divine Majesty may overtake it one day and it will bow down (collapse)", was the tenant's reply.[81]

One day while al-Jahiz (an ugly-faced renowned Arab scholar) was sitting at the door of his house, there came to him a woman and requested him to do her a favour by accompanying her to a place. Al-Jahiz went along with her till she reached the shop of a Jewish jeweller and said to the latter: "Like this". And then she left the place without saying anything to al-Jahiz. Greatly surprised, al-Jahiz asked the jeweller as to what she meant by saying "like this". The jeweller said: "The lady had earlier wanted me to engrave the image of a devil on the stone of her ring. But when I told her that I had no idea of the devil, she brought you here and told me what you have just heard".[82]

It is said that Abu al-Qasim al-Juhani, a judge and one of the friends of a certain minister, al-Muhallabi, was a habitual liar who would relate baseless and unacceptable news and stories. One day while he was sitting in the company of some people including Abu al-Faraj al-Isfahani, author of the encyclopaedic work, the *Kitab al-Aghani* (The Book of Songs), there took place a discussion on the mint plant as well as on its size and length. Al-Juhani participated in the discussion, saying: "In a particular country the mint plant grows as such a tall tree that ladders and a variety of household furnitures are made of its wood". Getting annoyed at this exaggerated statement, Abu al-Faraj said: "Yes, the wonders of the world are numerous; and the one which I am going to relate is stranger and more wonderful. It is that I am having a male pigeon which lays two eggs in the period of over twenty days and hatches them. Then I replace the eggs with two different sizes of balls of brass; and when the breeding period is over, the balls burst into a wash-basin and a water-jug". On hearing this, all those present there burst into laughter. While al-Juhani who perceived the intention of Abu al-Faraj refrained thenceforth from exaggerating his statements.[83]

Lastly, there flourished in the 'Abbasid period (750-1258 C.E.) a good number of professional poet-humorists also, who were popularly known as *al-Shu'ara al-Mujjan* (licentious poets). They also contributed a great deal to the enrichment of humour literature in Arabic by their poetical compositions. Abu Dulamah, Abu Nasr Kushajim, Ibn al-Hajjaj, Ibn Sakrah al-Hashimi, Abu al-Shamaqmaq, etc., were some such eminent poets. The following examples may be taken as sufficiently illustrative specimens of their style.

Abu Dulamah

Zand Ibn al-Jawn Abu Dulamah had his own style of entertaining Caliph al-Mahdi. He used to evoke his laughter by scoffing at himself, his wife and his other household members. It is said that one day he visited the caliph who was sitting in the company of such dignitaries as Isma'il bin Muhammad, 'Isa bin Musa, al-'Abbas bin Muhammad, Muhammad bin Ibrahim and a number of the Hashimite elite. The caliph ordered Abu Dulamah to satirise anyone of those present there. He also threatened him with cutting off his tongue in case he failed to do so. It was a very difficult situation for him, for he did not want to hurt the feelings of anyone of them. So, he had no alternative but to satirise himself in the following verses:

Let it be known to you, Abu Dulamah,

You neither belong to a noble people,

Nor do you have any nobility in you.

When you put on the turban, you appear like a monkey,

And when you put off the turban, you look like a swine.

You have combined in yourself both ugliness and meanness,

And meanness is always followed by ugliness.

If you happen to have obtained the worldly pleasure,

Don't shout, for the Day of Judgement is quite near at hand.[84]

The entire audience burst into laughter on hearing these verses, and rewarded Abu Dulamah heavily. He was also capable of employing his wit and humour on all possible occasions. It is said that Caliph al-Mahdi went out hunting one day along with 'Ali bin Sulayman and Abu Dulamah. The caliph shot at a deer and killed it. His companion 'Ali bin Sulayman also shot at a deer, but he missed the target and killed a hunting dog instead. The caliph laughed at it, and asked Abu Dulamah to versify the incident, whereupon the latter recited the following verses extempore:

Al-Mahdi shot at a deer and transpierced its heart with the arrow,

And 'Ali bin Sulayman (missing the target) shot at a hunting dog and killed it.

So congratulations to both of you, but everyone will eat his own provision.[85]

On hearing these verses, the caliph laughed and ordered for Abu Dulamah the reward of 30,000 *dirhams.*

Abu Nasr Kushajim

Abu Nasr Kushajim was another distinguished poet-humorist of his time who used to incite laughter by versifying the scenes of miserliness. For instance, once he was invited by one of his friends, who was known for his miserliness. As soon as they sat down to eat, both guest and host had a difficult job to perform. While the hungry guest tried to steal some morsels, the host intervened by resorting to various methods. The thoughts and ideas occuring in their minds on this occasion are brilliantly described by the poet as follows:

One of my most miserly friends as well as the most adept in the art of miserliness,

Invited me as a friend invites his friend, and I visited him as a friend visits his friend;

But when we sat down to eat, he felt as if I was eating of his flesh.

Sometimes, he would become angry, sometimes he would revile his servant.

I understood that both his anger and revilement were because of me,

So I started stealing morsels out of fear, but he kept me under his constant watch by his side-glances.

Whenever I extended my hand secretly to steal a morsel, he looked askance at me, and then I would busy myself with the vegetable.

Ultimately my hand committed a sin, for hunger had almost deprived me of my mind,

And when my hand gently pulled the chickens' leg for a while,

He himself pulled my leg as I had done the chickens' leg.

When he served sweets after the meal, my fate with it also was the same as it was earlier with the meal.

Then I stood up with the thought that had I remained hungry at home with the intention of fasting,

I would have got the reward of fasting.[86]

From what has been discussed above it is quite evident that humour was never considered a taboo in Islam even by its greatest religious authorities. Instead, they recommended it as indispensable and beneficial for the life of man. Thus, it was quite in line with the traditions of Islam that the Arab-Muslim scholars and scientists, who made tremendous contributions to all branches of knowledge and learning, did not spend all their time discussing serious matters. But they also knew how to temper their erudition with wit and humour. Being a sociable people, they enjoyed each other's company, listened to music, recited poetry, exchanged anecdotes, minted as well as appreciated good jokes and laughed heartily, thereby taking their full share of the human life.

References

1. *The Times of India*, New Delhi, June 23,1996.

2. *Ibid.* June 20, 1982.

3. Ibn 'Abd Rabbih, *al-'Iqd al-Farid (Fukahat wa Mulah)*, ed. by Karam al-Bustani, Beirut, p. 10.

4. *Ibid.*, p. 5.

5. *Ibid.*, p. 6.

6. *Ibid.*, p. 8.

7. *Ibid.*, pp. 8-9.

8. *Ibid.*, p. 9.

9. *The Jami Tirmidhi*, ed. with notes by Abdul Rahman Mubarakpuri, Delhi : Jayyid Barqi Press, Vol. III, 1352 A.H., p. 142.

10. *Ibid.*, p. 142.

11. Abu Ishaq Ibrahim bin 'Ali al-Husri al-Qayrawani, *Jam'al Jawahir fi'l Mulah wa'l-Nawadir*, ed. by 'Ali Muhammad al-Bajawi, 1953, p. 36.

12. *Ibid.*, p. 36.

13. Ibn al-Jawzi, *Akhbar al-Hamqa' wa'l-Mughaffalin*, Beirut, p. 21.

14. 'Ali bin Abi Talib (d. 661 C.E.) was son-in-law of Prophet Muhammad (P.B.H.), the first Shi'ah Imam and the fourth *Rashidi* caliph.

15. Ibn al-Jawzi, *op. cit.*, p. 17.

16. Abu Ishaq al-Qayrawani, *op. cit.*, p. 35.

17. Usamah bin Zayd (615-674 C.E.) was a venerable *Companion* of the Prophet (P.B.H.). He was also the narrator of 128 Apostolic Traditions.

18. Ibn al-Jawzi, *op. cit.*, p. 17.

19. Abu al-Darda (d. 652 C.E.), a renowned *Companion*, was described by the Prophet (P.B.H.) as the wise man of the *Ummat* (the Muslim community). He was the narrator of 179 Apostolic Traditions. He was appointed as *qadi* (judge) of Damascus by Caliph 'Umar bin al-Khattab.

20. Ibn Hazm, *Tawq al-Hamamah*, ed. by Faruq Sa'd, Beirut, 1992, 53.

21. 'Amr ibn al-'As (574-664 C.E.), a Companion of the Prophet (P.B.H.), was one of the most distinguished generals produced by Islam.

22. Ibn 'Abd Rabbih, *Op. cit.*, p. 7.

23. Muhammad bin Muslim al-Zuhri (678-742 C.E.); a *Tabi'i* (follower of the Prophet's *Companions*), was held in high esteem for his knowledge of the Qur'an, Apostolic traditions and jurisprudence. He was a. great religious authority of his time.

24. Ibn al-Jawzi, *op. cit.*, p. 17.

25. 'Umar bin 'Abd al-'Aziz (681-720 C.E.) was a pious and just Umayyad ruler. He is also known as the fifth *Rashidi* caliph.

26. Ibn 'Abd Rabbih, *op. cit.*, p. 6.

27. Hisham bin 'Abd al-Malik (690-743 C.E.) was a distinguished Umayyad ruler and statesman.

28. Ibn 'Abd Rabbih, *op. cit.*, p. 7.

29. Ibn 'Abd-Rabbih (860-940 C.E.) was the most distinguished author of Muslim Spain in the domain of literature. His *al-'Iqd al-Farid* is one of the few most important works on the literary history of the Arabs.

30. Ibn 'Abd Rabbih, *op. cit.*, p. 5.

31. Abu Hayyan al-Tawhidi (d. 1010 C.E.) was a distinguished Arab litterateur and philosopher who flourished in the 'Abbasid period.

32. Abu Hayyan al-Tawhidi, *al-Basa'ir wa al-Dhakha'ir*, ed. by Dr. Ibrahim al-Kilani, Damascus, Vol. I, pp. 60-61.

33. Abu Hayyan al-Tawhidi, *al-Imta' wa al-Mu'anasah*, ed. by Dr. Ahmad Amin, Cairo, Vol. II, p. 50.

34. *Akhbar al-Hamqa wa'l-Mughaffalin*, *op. cit.*, p. 46.

35. *Ibid.*, p. 47.

36. Hikmat Beg Sharif, *Nawadir Juha al-Kubra*, al-Maktabah al-Tijariyah, Egypt, p. 86.

37. 'Abd al-Sattar Ahmad al-Farraj, *Akhbar Juha*, Egypt, p. 164.

38. *Ibid.*

39. Ash'ab Bin Jubayr (d. 771 C.E.) was born and brought up in Madinah. A client of Caliph 'Uthman, he lived a long life and saw the period of the *Companions* of the Prophet (P.B.H.) as well as those of the *Tabi'in* (followers of the *Companions*) and the *Tab' Tabi'in* (followers of the followers of the *Companions*). He also visited Baghdad in the reign of the 'Abbasid Caliph, al-Mansur, and lived there upto the time of Caliph al-Mahdi. He was very greedy and sharpminded, and had a ready retort to everything.

40. *The New Arab*, Vol. V (October 1978), Delhi, p. 44.

41. Muhammad bin Shakir Bin Ahmad al-Kutubi, *Fawat all A'yan*, p. 40.

42. *Ibid.*, p. 40.

43. The holy Qur'an, XI:79 (tr. by A. Yusuf Ali).

44. *Jam' al-Jawahir, op. cit.*, p. 68.

45. 'Abd Allah Ibn 'Umar (613-692 C.E.) was a pious and renowned *Companion* of the Prophet (P.B.H.). He was the last *Companion* to die in Makkah. He was also the narrator of 2630 Apostolic Traditions.

46. *Fukahat wa Mulah, op. cit.*, p. 84.

47. Ibn Hajar al-'Asqalani, *Lisan al-Mizan*, India, 1329 A.H., Vol. I, p. 451.

48. Abu Nuwas (d. 810 C.E.) was the celebrated boon-companion and court jester of Caliph Harun al-Rashid. He was a gifted poet, whose genius, in the words of R.A. Nicholson, was most brilliantly inspired by the two motives of love and wine.

49. Mahmud Kamil Farid, *Diwan Abi Nuwas*, Egypt, p. 37.

50. *Ibid.*, pp. 56-57.

51. *Jam' al-Jawahir, op. cit.*, p. 249.

52. Muzayyid was a distinguished wit; who flourished in the time of Caliph al-Mahdi.

53. *Al Imta' wa'l-Mu'anasah, op. cit.*, Vol. II, p. 55.

54. *Jam' al-Jawahir, op. cit.*, p. 307.

55. *Ibid.*, p. 307.

56. Abu al-Ayna' (d. 895 C.E.) flourished as an eminent humorist of his time in Baghdad. Caliph al-Mutawakkil was greatly impressed by his eloquence, presence of mind and witty remarks. He lost his eyesight at the age of forty. But his blindness did not come in the way of his rising into prominence. He was always found to be very bold and full of confidence in himself

57. Abu'l Hasan 'Ali bin Muhammad al-Shabushti, *Kitab al Diyarat*, p. 232.

58. Yaqut, *Mu'jam al-Udaba*, Egypt, Vol. XVIII, p. 290.

59. *Ibid.*, p. 293.

60. *Ibid.*, p. 302.

61. Al-Jahiz, *al-Bukhala*, ed. by Taha al-Hajiri, Egypt, 1958, p. 26.

62. *Al-'Iqd. al-Farid* (*al-Majanin wa'l-Bukhala wa'l-Tufayliyun*), ed. by Karam al-Bustani, Beirut, p. 88.

63. *Jam'al-Jawahir, op. cit.*, p. 308.

64. *Al-Majanin wa'l-Bukhala wa'l-Tufayliyun, op. cit.*, pp. 128-129.

65. *Jam' al-Jawahir, op. cit.*, pp. 204-5.

66. *Ibid.* p. 161.

67. The Arab Journal *Al-'Arabi*, No. 97 (December 1966), Kuwait, pp. 154-55.

68. *Al-Arabi, op. cit.*, No. 208 (March 1986), p. 60.

69. *Akhbar al-Hamqa wa'l-Mughaffalin, op. cit.*, p. 52.

70. *Ibid.*, p. 161.

71. *Ibid.*, p. 161.

72. *Fakahat wa Mulah, op. cit.*, p. 107.

73. *Al-Imta 'wa'l-Mu'anasah, op. cit.*, Vol. II, p. 58.

74. Al-Khatib al-Bhaghdadi, *al-Tatfil*, p. 35.

75. *Ibid.*, p. 64.

76. *Al-Majanin wa'l-Bukhala wa'l-Tufayliyun, op. cit.*, pp. 156-57.

77. *Ibid.*, pp. 158-59.

78. Ibn Qutaybah, *'Uyun-ul-Akhbar*, Vol. IV, p. 44.

79. Ahmad Shihabuddin al-Qalyubi, *Nawadir al-Qalyubi*, Egypt, 1320 A.H., p. 155.

80. *Al-Arabi, op. cit.*, No. 141 (August 1970), p. 33.

81. *Al-Arabi*, No. 169 (December 1972), p 32.

82. *Nawadir al-Jahiz*, ed. by Jamil Jabr, Beirùt, 1955, p. 19.

83. *Al-Arabi*, No. 180 (November 1973), p. 115.

84. *Jam' al-Jawahir, op. cit.*, p. 111.

85. *Ibid.*, p. 112.

86. Dr. Tawfiq al-Fil: *"Shi'r al-Idhak 'ind al-'Arab"*, in *al-'Arabi, op. cit.*, No. 323.

10

Islam : The Concept of Punishment

A lot of hue and cry is raised by Western writers on Islamic provisions regarding punishment. In continuous chain of misrepresentation they hold them as uncivilized, inhuman and barbaric. They go so far as to declare that unless Islam is prepared to relent on these and other legal provisions of the *Shari'ah* "there can and will be no accommodation; only a continuation of Western rejection of Islam".[1]

The Islamic concept of punishment differs fundamentally from the individualistic and communist theories of punishment. The capitalist Western states based on individualistic philosophy of life go to extreme limits in sanctifying the individual. They regard him as the centre of all social life. They show undue sympathy to criminals by holding them as victims of adverse circumstances, psychological complexes and nervous disorders. Freud was the champion of this theory based on psycho-analysis. All the psychoanalysts who came after him believed in "psychological determinism", according to which man has no freedom of will or action. He is, therefore, bound to act in a predetermined manner. Thus, he is entitled for sympathy and kind treatment rather than punishment for his crimes.

On the other hand, communism refers offences to economic rather than psychological factors. Economic conditions do have a great impact on the feelings and actions of individuals, but it is wrong to say that human conduct is influenced and guided by economic factors alone. Nevertheless, Communist countries inflict severe penalties on individuals who rebel against the state which is considered as a sacred entity.[2]

Although, there is partial truth in both individualistic and communist conceptions of human nature regarding crime, they are based on faulty hypothesis. It is true that circumstances and economic conditions do have a great impact on the behaviour and personality of an individual, but he is not created as a helpless puppet in their hands He is endowed with a tremendous controlling energy which enables him to hold fast to the path of righteousness against all heavy odds. Hence, he is held responsible for the crimes committed by him. This is described in the Qur'an as *amanat* or tust given to man. It is the same trust which makes man superior to all other creatures of the universe. Consider the following Verses:

> "Lo ! We offered the trust unto the heavens and the earth and the hills, but they shrank from bearing it and were afraid of it. And man assumed it. Lo! he hath proved a tyrant and a fool".[3]

> "So Allah punisheth hypocritical men and hypocritical women and idolatrous men and

idolatrous women. But Allah pardoneth believing men and believing women, and Allah is Forgiving and Merciful".[4]

Islam never prescribes punishments haphazardly. It combines the best of the communist as well as the individualistic theories of punishment in accordance with the dictates of sound logic and wise reasoning by taking into consideration all conditions and circumstances connected with the offence. 'Acts are determined by motives', is a saying of the Prophet.

Islam strives to bring about peace and order in society by holding man accountable for his actions on the Day of Judgment as well as by means of punitive legislation. As such the fear of punishment in the Hereafter has proved an effective deterrent against evil. The very idea that 'Allah knows what the soul of man whispers to him, and that He is nearer to him than his jugular vein',[5] is enough to strike terror in the heart of Allah-fearing man and make him just, self-disciplined and law-abiding.

Preventive Punishments

Islam prescribes preventive punishments for crimes of grave magnitude such as murder, physical injury, adultery, theft, columny and gambling, etc. in order to deter individuals from committing them. Even in respect of these crimes the Islamic Law is not coercive but corrective and persuasive. Moreover, it does not carry out such punishments unless it is proved that the criminal was not acting under any compulsive obligation.

Islam has a two-fold mission in this connection. First, it diminishes the scope for crimes by taking all possible measures and safeguards. Secondly, it prescribes exemplary punishments for crimes committed in a healthy society in spite of the safeguards. For example, a healthy society based on Islamic principles is bound to provide the basic needs of all individuals. It is responsible for the maintenance of all such persons who are unable to earn livelihood. Hence, the compulsory payment of zakat in Islam for the benefit of such persons. But even after all these safeguards if someone commits theft, he is given an exemplary punishment as described in the Qur'an:

> "As for the thief, both male and female, cut off their hands. It is the reward of their own deeds, an exemplary punishment from Allah. Allah is Mighty. Wise".[6]

But such punishment is not carried out if it is proved that he was impelled to theft by hunger.

Similarly, Islam is fully aware of the gravity of the crime of adultery in society. It is, not only highly immoral, but also cuts at the very roots of the family life. Since Islam gives maximum importance to marriage and family, it has prohibited all forms of sexual deviation and pre- or extra-marital sex. It has sought to achieve this objective by evolving various methods to curb temptation towards sex outside marriage. It has encouraged all to get married, legalised limited polygamy, and prescribed various regulations regarding dress for women and social mixing of the sexes. Another important measure taken by it to curb adultery is that it awards the most horrible punishment for it. "The adulteress and the adulterer, flog each one of them with a hundred lashes", says the Qur'an.[7] The punishment for the married adulterer and the adulteress is that they should be stoned to death, according to a tradition of the Prophet.

These sentences are certainly very harsh, but still more strict are the procedures laid down to be observed before an accused person may be convicted. That is the main reason why such punishments have been very rarely executed in the history of Islam. Four eyewitnesses are needed to substantiate the crime. The benefit of doubt is always given to the accused. Prophet Muhammad has described it saying, "to let nine criminals go free is preferable to convicting one innocent man".

Likewise, Islam is fully aware of the danger posed to the morals of a society by rumour-mongers. It has discouraged all frivolous talk about sexual relations by prescribing stringent penalties for accusers of chaste women, as described in the Qur'an: "And those who accuse honourable women but bring not four witnesses, flog them with eighty lashes and never accept their testimony. They indeed ere evil-doers".[8]

The Law of Retaliation (Qisas)

Apart from stringent punishments for crimes mentioned above, Islam also provides for the principle of *qisas* (retaliation). When someone causes a physical injury or harm, the injured person is given the right of equal requital. This finds legitimacy in the following Verses of the Qur'an:

> "O ye who believe ! Retaliation is prescribed for you in the matter of the murdered; the freeman for the freeman, and the slave for the slave, and the female for the female. And for him who is forgiven somewhat by his injured brother, prosecution according to usage and payment unto him in kindness. This is an alleviation and a mercy from your Lord. He who transgresseth after this will have a painful doom".[9]

> "And We prescribed for them therein: The life for the life, and the eye for the eye, and the nose for the nose, and the ear for the ear, and the tooth for the tooth, and for wounds retaliation. But whoso forgoeth it (in the way of charity) it shall be expiation for him. Whoso judgeth not by that which Allah hath revealed: such are wrong-doers".[10]

> "And there is life for you in retaliation, O men of understanding, that ye may ward off evil".[11]

Contrary to the charges levelled by critics against the Qur'anic procedure of retaliation, it not only meets the strict claims of justice, but also shuts the door to private vengeance, the consequences of which are always most horrible. While legalising retaliation, the Qur'an highly recommends the act of forgiveness. The aggrieved party is persuaded to forgo his right to retaliation by forgiving, or by consenting to accept a reasonable compensation instead. Besides, retaliation is allowed only in cases of wilful destruction of life. If there is the least doubt regarding the wilful character of the offence, retaliation will not be applicable in that case.[12]

It is important to note that in the administration of justice as well as execution of deterrent punishments, no distinction is made between the privileged and the unprivileged. This is fully substantiated by the case of a certain woman belonging to a respected family of the Quraish, who was found guilty of theft. Some prominent people including Asma, daughter of Zaid, interceded with Prophet Muhammad to save her from the punishment. But the Prophet refused to condone the crime, saying:

"Many a community ruined itself in the past as they only punished the poor and ignored the offences of the exalted. By God, if Muhammad's daughter Fatima would have committed theft, her hand would have been severed".[13]

Lastly, it may be said in conclusion that the penalties prescribed by Islam are more of a functional nature, to regulate and deter. They are rightly called *hudud* (limits), which are incurred as a consequence of crossing the limits set by Allah for the overall benefit of man himself in a society based on the Islamic principles of morality. The Islamic provisions for punishment are more concerned with deterring individuals from committing crime than with punishing them. Thus, it can be rightly claimed for Islam that it has tackled the problem of crime in society both efficiently and mercifully.

References

1. Khurram J. Murad: "Shri'ah, the Way of justice", published in the *Muslim World League Journal*, Vol. XIII, No. 1, p. 9.
2. Muhammad Qutb: *Islam, the Misunderstood Religion*, 246.
3. The Qur'an: (XXXIII: 72), tr. by M.M. Pickthall.
4. *Ibid.*, (XXXIII: 73), tr. by M.M. Pickthall.
5. Dr. Muslehuddin: *Philosophy of Islamic Law and the Orientalists*, p. 109.
6. The Qur'an: (V: 38), tr. by M.M. Pickthall.
7. The Qur'an: (XXIV: 2).
8. The Qur'an: (XXIV: 4).

9. The Qur'an: (II: 178.), tr. by M.M. Pickthall.
10. *Ibid.*, (V: 45), tr. by M.M. Pickthall.
11. *Ibid.*, (II: 179), tr. by M.M. Pickthall.
12. M. Muslehuddin, *op. cit.*, p. 114.
13. Quoted by Athar Husain in his *Prophet Muhammad and his Mission*, p. 141.

11

Legitimacy of Fresh Judgement in Islam

It is true that the commandments of Allah as described in the Qur'an and elaborated in the Sunnah (the words and deeds of Prophet Muhammad) relating to ritual and worshiping, civil and legal obligations and punishments, have been made binding on the Muslims; and there is little scope for independent judgment in respect of them. Allah says: "Perfected is the way of thy Lord. There is naught that can change His words. He is the Hearer, the Knower".[1] These fundamental principles and rules constitute the basic structure of *Din* (*i.e.*, the religion of Islam) which is changeless and perfect from the Muslim's point of view.

But the Islamic *Shari'at* (Law) which consists of laws and by-laws governed by the fundamental principles of Islam, is not at all static, stationary and immobile. It is rather dynamic, adaptable, flexible and accommodative. It is, therefore, fully competent to meet the legal challenges of all times to come for the benefit of humanity at large. It is remarkable to note that while the core of *Din* has been basically the same right from the 'descent' of Adam on earth down to the age of Prophet Muhammad, *Shari'at* has been changing and developing according to the requirements of different ages. This position is made quite clear in the following Verses:

> "He hath ordained for you that religion which He commended unto Noah, and that which We inspire in thee (Muhammad), and that which he commended unto Abraham and Moses and Jesus, saying: Establish the religion, and be not divided therein."[2]

> "And unto thee have We revealed the Scripture with the truth, confirming whatever Scripture was before it, and a watcher over it. So judge between them by that which Allah hath revealed, and follow not their desires away from the truth which hath come unto thee. For each We have appointed a divine law and a traced-out way."[3]

It is clear from the above Verses that every Prophet was sent with a two-fold mission: (a) to testify *Din* taught by his predecessors, and (b) to make certain changes and amendments in the Law given by the Prophet before him. So Jesus declared at the time of his advent: "I have come to you confirming that which was before me of the Torah and to legalise some of that which was forbidden to you".[4] But since Muhammad was the last Prophet and the Qur'an the last Revealed Book, there is the provision for *ijtihad* (exercise of independent judgment) in Islam, in order to solve such problems as are not covered by the Qur'an and the Sunnah. That is the main reason that while *Din* is declared as completed by Allah through Prophet Muhammad, no such announcement is made in respect of *Shari'at*. So *Shari'at* is an everdeveloping process. As such at no stage of its history it can be said to be in its final shape. The concept of *ijtihad* keeps the evolutionary spirit of Muslim jurisprudence alive. It has its roots in a well-known Verse of the Qur'an[5]—"As for those who strive in Us, We surely guide them to Our paths, and Lo! Allah is with the good".[6] It is more clearly expressed in the following conversation between the Prophet and his appointee as governor of Yemen, Mu'adh ibn Jabal, which sums up the Magna Charta of Islamic legal fundamentals:

The Prophet : "How will you conduct yourself when a question arises?"

Mu'adh : "According to the Book of Allah".

The Prophet : "But if you do not find the solution therein"?

Mu'adh : "According to the practice of the Prophet".

The Prophet : "And if you do not find the solution in it also ?"

Mu'adh : "Then I shall apply my own reasoning".

On hearing this, the Prophet applauded the governor on his reply to apply his private judgment in case of such matters as are not covered by the Qur'an and the Sunnah.

Scope and Method of Ijtihad

The word *ijtihad* is derived from the Arabic root 'Jahd' meaning 'exert'. In the terminology of Islamic Law it means to exert with a view to forming an independent judgment on a legal question. As described above, there can be no question of resorting to *ijtihad* in matters explicitly dealt with in the Qur'an and the Sunnah, such as the obligation of prayers, fasting, zakat, hajj, law of inheritance, prohibition of wine and adultery, etc.

The Islamic legal system called *fiqh* was primarily based on the Qur'an and the Sunnah. The Qur'an consists of 114 small and big chapters. Of about six thousand Verses in the Qur'an only about two hundred thirty-six, most of which occur in the Medinese portion, especially chapters two and four, may be classed as strictly legislative. As stated in the Qur'an, the Verses are of two kinds: (a) Verses which are clear revelations, and (b) others which bear allegorical meaning. This implies that there is scope for further interpretations of the Verses belonging to the second category in consonance with the spirit of Islam.

The Sunnah is the second greatest source of Islamic Law. So long as the Prophet lived, he was the sole law-giver. His words and deeds constituted the law. His role as interpreter of the Quran is described as follows:

> "And We have revealed unto thee the Remembrance that thou mayst explain to mankind that which hath been revealed for them, and that haply they may reflect".[7]

Similarly, the Prophet's status as law-giver is illustrated in the following Verse:

> "He will enjoin on them that which is right and forbid them that which is wrong. He will make lawful for

them all good things and prohibit for them only the foul; and he will relieve them of their burden and the fetters that they used to wear.[8]

Later on, after the expansion of Islam in Syria, Iraq, Egypt, Iran and other conquered territories, it soon became evident that these primary sources were not sufficient to meet the requirements of new cases—civil, criminal, political and financial. Hence the necessity for speculation. This gave rise to two new fundamental principles: *qiyas, i.e.,* analogical deduction, and *ijma, i.e.,* consensus of the community. The difference between them is that while *qiyas* is individual discretion based on analogical deduction rather than on free use of reason, *ijma* is collective consensus of the community. The concept of *ijma'* finds legitimacy in a tradition of the Prophet :

"My community will never unite in error".[9]

It is remarkable to note that the judgments derived on the basis of the first two sources are recognised as absolute and infallible, while the decisions arrived at through *ijtihad* based on the remaining two sources are not considered as infallible.

This is a very significant point which suggests that the decisions derived through *ijtihad* are subject to change and amendment for the better.

In the course of time various other principles and methods of *ijtihad* were devised to meet the changing needs of newly converted Muslims. Technically, they were called *istidlal* (inference), *istihsan* (preference), and *istislah* or *al-masalih-ul-mursalah* (public good), etc.

Istidlal is expression of the connection that exists between one proposition and another. For instance, sale is a contract, and the basis of every contract is consent; therefore consent is the basis of sale. It is a sort of logical deduction for finding a basis for a rule.[10]

Istihsan and *al-masalih-ul-mursalah* stand for freedom in the use of one's reason. This theory was enunciated by Imam Abu Hanifah who represented the school of the people of *ra'y* (opinion). Commenting upon *istihsan* and *al-masalih-ul-mursalah,* Macdonald says: "*Istihsan* is the one that the legist, in spite of the fact that the analogy of the fixed code clearly points out to one course, considers it better to follow a different one; and the other (*al-masalih-ul-mursalah*) is that under the same conditions, he chooses a free course, for the sake of the general benefit to the community". While *istihsan* is equivalent to equity in the English sense, *istislah* corresponds to utility which forms the basis of legislation in the modern world.[11] Although opposed by some scholars like Ibn-ul-Qayyim and Imam-Shafi'i, it was fully approved by Imam Malik. This theory is based on the conception that *Shari'ah* is for social utility, and that its main function is to promote welfare of man by preventing evil.

Customs and social manners of a community were also taken into consideration while formulating laws and rules for it. Besides, welfare of man, establishment of peace and justice and promotion of wisdom, etc., also count in Islamic legislation. Since these are the supreme objectives of Islam, the doors for legislating laws in order to realise them are always open for the Muslims.

Independent Thinking

During the days of Prophet Muhammad and the first four Caliphs independent thinking was encouraged. As described above, the Prophet exhorted his followers that they should apply their minds to solve their problems. He himself resorted to *ijtihad* in the absence of any clear injunction from Allah regarding a problem. He welcomed honest difference of opinion, saying: "The difference of opinion in my *Ummah* (community) is a sign of bounty of my Lord".

Likewise, the first four Caliphs often exercised their own judgment in many matters. They followed the principles of analogy and consensus in extracting rules of law from the texts of the Qur'an and the Sunnah. The very first problem that confronted the Companions was the election of Abu Bakr to the Caliphate. But prior to his death, the Prophet had asked Abu Bakr to lead prayers. That was taken by them as a sufficient ground to appoint him as their leader on the analogy that the one who is their leader in religious matters, must be their head in worldly affairs also. Another glaring act of *ijtihad* is to be found in Caliph 'Umar's suspension of the penalty for theft in time of famine. Although there is clear Qur'anic injunction to cut off the hands of the thief, yet the Caliph suspended it in the year of famine because of necessity and in order that people might keep alive. Similarly, workers and manufacturers such as tailors and goldsmiths were not responsible for the loss of things given to them. But when Caliph Ali argued that if they are not held responsible, they will become negligent with the result that the owners will have to suffer a great loss, a rule was immediately enacted to that effect by consensus.[12] Such was the juristic freedom in Islam.

Ijtihad by the Four Great Jurists of Islam

Among the jurists who fashioned the whole Islamic legal system, or *corpus juris*, the four founders of juristic schools deserve special mention, namely, Nu'man ibn Thabit Abu

Hanifah (d. 150 A.H.), Abu Abdullah Malik ibn Anas (d. 179 A.H.), Muhammad ibn Idris al-Shafi'i (d. 204 A.H.) and Ahmad ibn Hanbal (d. 241 A.H.). They were all jurists of outstanding scholarship and learning.

Of the above jurists who contributed a great deal to the evolution of Muslim jurisprudence, Imam Abu Hanifah was the most prominent and influential. It is a well-known fact that the traditions of Prophet Muhammad had not been codified by the time of the Imam. Only seventeen traditions are said to have reached him. He, therefore, built his legal system on his private judgment. The principle of *istihsan* (preference) enunciated by him is in fact a recognition of local conditions. It led him to ignore, under certain conditions, even a precedent handed down from earlier generations of legists. To quote his own words: "The analogy in this case points to such and such a rule, but under the circumstances I hold it better to rule thus and thus". What differentiates the Hanafite system from the other legal systems of Islam, *i.e.*, the Malikite, the Hanbalite and the Shafiite, is the fact that while the latter lacked elasticity and adhered too literally to the texts of the Qur'an and the traditions, the former was marked by a great deal of liberalism and elasticity. It also took into consideration the local and changed conditions of life. This principle made his system popular all over the Muslim world. Almost one half of the world of Sunnite Islam adheres to his system of religio-juridical thought which the German Orientalist von Kremer has applauded as "the highest and loftiest achievement of which Islam was capable".[13] He is reported to have elucidated eighty-three thousand juristic-theological issues of which thirty-eight thousand pertained to acts of devotion and prayer and forty-five thousand to transactions, rights and duties owed by one Muslim to another. The total number of his legal opinions was six hundred thousand.[14]

The founders of the other legal systems also tried to meet new conditions in their own way, notwithstanding the fact that they differed among themselves on certain points. *Al-Mudawwanah*, the collection of religious and judicial sentences of Malik ibn Anas, contains thirty-six thousand decisions. The collection of writings and lectures of al-Shafi'i entitled *Kitab-ul-Umm* runs into seven bulky volumes, while the decisions of Ahmed ibn Hanbal were compiled by Abu Bakr Khallal (d. 311 A.H.) into forty volumes.[15]

All the four schools of Muslim jurisprudence are considered by Muslims as true and faithful. But after the establishment of these schools, into which the whole Muslim community divided itself, the doors of *ijtihad* were considered to be closed forever to the Muslims. This gave rise to the doctrine of *taqlid*, *i.e.* to follow without question the decisions reached in the past was the correct and right thing to do for the believers. The followers of this doctrine called "Conformists" made the Muslim jurisprudence static by maintaining that the believers must follow the rulings of the learned and the learned must follow the great jurists of the past. According to them, such obedience was good, while questioning such obedience was bad. But that was a sad development in the history of Islam. It only denotes the lethargy that had overtaken the decadent Muslim world. Its main defect was that it virtually extinguished the practice of looking directly at the original sources of the religion for legal guidance. Moreover, the four recognised jurists never claimed finality for themselves. That was the main reason why a number of Muslim thinkers opposed the doctrine of *taqlid*. Taqiduddin Ibn Taymiyah (d. 1328 A.D.) was the first eminent Muslim theologian who raised his voice against the doctrine of *taqlid*. He was a *mujtahid*, and took a number of legal decisions by following the principles of *ijtihad*. In the sixteenth century Jalaluddin al-Suyuti claimed the same privilege of *ijtihad* to which he added the idea of a renovator at the beginning of each century. The eighteenth century saw the rise of Muhammad Ibn Abdul Wahhab who rose in revolt against the finality of schools, and vigorously asserted the right of private judgment. Besides, Muhammad bin Ali al-Shawkani, Muhammad Abduhu, Jamaluddin al-Afghani, Shah Waliullah of Delhi, Sir Sayyid Ahmad Khan, Allamah Iqbal and Syed Ameer Ali, etc., also asserted the right of *ijtihad* for the Muslims in their respective places and times. For instance, Allamah Iqbal refuted the practice of *taqlid* by telling that it was contrary to the inner impulse of Islam. He encouraged Muslim nations to follow the example of Turkey in modernising themselves in the following words:

> "The truth is that among the Muslim nations of today, Turkey alone has shaken off its dogmatic slumber, and attained to self-consciousness. She alone has claimed her right of intellectual freedom; she alone has passed from the ideal to the real—a transition which entails keen intellectual and moral struggle. To her the growing complexities of a mobile and broadening life are sure to bring new situations suggesting new points of view, and necessitating fresh interpretations of principles which are only of an academic interest to a people who have never experienced the joy of spiritual expansion. It is, I think, the English thinker Hobbes who makes this

acute observation that to have a succession of identical thoughts and feelings is to have no thoughts and feelings at all. Such is the lot of most Muslim countries today. They are mechanically repeating old values, whereas the Turk is on the way to creating new values."[16]

The above account of the various aspects and prospects of *ijtihad* clearly proves that its doors are as wide open today as they might have been in the times of Prophet Muhammad and early Caliphs. Thus, the Muslims are equipped with the most effective tool for framing fresh laws to suit the modern conditions of life as well as to solve all such problems that may confront them in the near or distant future with a view to promoting human happiness and prosperity in accordance with the spirit of Islam.

References

1. The Qur'an: (VI: 116).
2. The Qur'an: (XLII: 13), tr. by M.M. Pickthall.
3. The Qur'an (V: 48), tr. by M.M. Pickthall.
4. The Qur'an: (III : 50).
5. Dr. M. Iqbal : *The Reconstruction of Religious Thought in Islam*, p. 148.
6. The Qur'an: (XXIX: 69), tr. by M.M. Pickthall.
7. The Qur'an: (XVI: 44).
8. *Ibid.*, VII: 157, tr. by M.M. Pickthall.
9. Quoted by Rafiq Zakaria in his article "Islam in a Changing World", pub. in the *Times of India, op. cit.*, July 12,1983, New Delhi.

10. Dr. M. Muslehuddin: *Philosophy of Islamic Law and the Orientalists*, p. 148.

11. *Ibid.*, pp. 152-53.

12. *Ibid.*, p. 134.

13. Kulturgeschichte, Vol. I, p. 497.

14. *The Muslim World League Journal*, Vol. XIII, No. 1, p. 21.

15. *Ibid.*, p. 21.

16. Dr. Muhammad Iqbal: *The Reconstruction of Religious thought in Islam*, p. 162.

12

Secular Dimensions of Islam for Peaceful Co-existence in Pluralistic Societies

The term secular or secularism originated in Europe in the later medieval period. In early medieval times in Europe there was a strong tendency among religious persons to despise worldly affairs and to meditate on God and on the life hereafter. Reaction to this medieval tendency took the form of a movement which has been in progress during the entire period of modern history. It was also looked upon as anti-Christian and anti-religious.

Later, in the second half of the twentieth century there took place a change in the religious attitude of Christian authorities, who advocated a sort of compromise or give and take. They held that man should not be concerned exclusively with the sacred, metaphysical and otherwordly aspects of life. He should rather get an opportunity to promote Christian values in his day-to-day life. To pursue human aspirations was no longer considered as anti-Christian and anti-religious.

In the Indian context as well as in the context of the present-day international scenario, this term is used to imply several things such as non-discrimination on the basis of caste, creed and colour, absence of dogmatism, bigotry and violence in religious matters, non-imposition of religious doctrines on others in socio-cultural, political and civilizational relations in pluralistic societies.

The secular and ethical framework of Islam for peaceful co-existence in pluralistic societies comprises tolerance, freedom of faith end conscience, the concept of universal brotherhood of mankind, sanctity of pacts and agreements made with others as well as universally accepted principles of humanism. Since here it is not possible to deal with all major points relating to the civilizational framework of Islam within the limited scope of this chapter, the Islamic basis for socio-political relations with non-Muslims on secular lines is briefly introduced below.

The Qur'anic Concept of Universal Brotherhood

One major hurdle in the way of peaceful co-existence is the false notion of racial superiority. It has already caused a great deal of bloodshed among different human races. But the Qur'an demolished the age-old structure of racial superiority by asserting the common origin of all human beings. It recognises piety end righteousness as the sole basis of nobility and superiority. This concept not only develops in man an optimistic attitude towards life by inspiring him to attain superiority through noble deeds, but also makes possible the realization of the universal brotherhood of mankind. This point is elaborately emphasized in the following verses:

يـا ايهـا الـنـاس إنـا خـلـقناكم من ذكروانثىٰ وجعلناكم شعوبا
وقبـائـل لتـعـارفـوا، ان اكـرمـكم عندالله اتقاكم، ان الله عليم
خبير۔

> O mankind Lo! We have created you male and female, and have made you nations and tribes that you may know one another. Lo ! The noblest of you in the sight of Allah is the best in conduct. Lo ! Allah is the Knower, Aware.[1]

كان الناس امة واحدة......

> Mankind were one community.[2]

Another important point to be noted in this connection is that the Qur'an is addressed not to a particular people, but to the whole mankind. This is evident from the fact that the word "Muslim" has occurred only 42 times in it, while the words "mankind" and "man" have occurred as many as 240 and 65 times respectively. This clearly shows that welfare of the whole mankind is one of the principal concerns of Islam.

That the Qur'anic concept of the universal brotherhood of mankind is not an unattainable ideal is established by the historical fact that Islam during the lifetime of the Prophet Muhammad had already seen that brotherhood which welded high and low, rich and poor, white and black into one fraternity, members of which forgot their racial differences and worked together as good Muslims ought in the service of humanity. Even persons belonging to lower strata of society, of whatever origin, were readily absorbed as equal members of the fraternity. The history of Islam is replete with examples of such persons reaching the highest positions. They were entrusted with prestigious offices of governors and military commanders. The Prophet Muhammad himself appointed Zaid, earlier a slave, as commander of the Muslim army. With a view to making such leadership effective, the Prophet addressed his followers, saying:

> Hear and obey (the orders of your leaders) although the man appointed above you as your leader be a

> negro-slave with a raisinlike head so long as he continues to enforce among you the laws of Allah.[3]

It was the exemplary realization of this objective of Islam which prompted the noted historian Arnold Toynbee to write in his *Civilization on Trial* that "the extinction of race consciousness between Muslims is one of the outstanding moral achievements of Islam, and in the contemporary world, there is, as it happens, a crying need for the propagation of this Islamic virtue."

Peace-loving Aspect of Muslim Behaviour

Another important measure taken by Islam in preparing the ground for communal harmony, an essential precondition for socio-cultural cohesion and understanding, is that it enjoins its followers to be peace-loving and non-aggressive. One distinctive sign of the Muslims is that whenever they meet, they greet one another by exchanging the message of peace, *i.e.*, by calling *assalamu 'alaikum* (peace be upon you). Besides, the Qur'an has sought to impress upon them the importance of peace in life by describing it in the following verses as one of the highest rewards that await virtuous men in paradise:

اولئك يجزون الغرفة بما صبروا ويلقون فيها تحية وسلاما۔

> They will be awarded the high place for as much as they were steadfast, and they will meet therein with welcome and the word of peace.[4]

لايسمعون فيها لغوا ولا تاثيما إلا قيلا سلاما سلاما۔

> There hear they no vain speaking nor recrimination, naught but the saying : peace and again peace.[5]

It is with a view to restraining their aggressive temper that mankind in general and Muslims in particular have been urged time and again through numerous Qur'nic verses to shun all kinds of aggression and oppression. Even in the event of being addressed and confronted by foolish and mischievous people they are advised to maintain peace by disposing of them in a polite manner. This is exactly what the following verse impresses upon Muslims:

وعباد الرحمن الذين يمشون على الأرض هونا وإذا خاطبهم الجاهلون قالوا سلاما.

> The faithful slaves of the Beneficent are they who walk upon the earth modestly, and when the foolish ones address them, answer : peace.[6]

The Qur'an not only exhorts Muslims to be just, humane, tolerant and sociable, but also warns them against the evil consequences of practising injustice and transgression by narrating to them tales of the ancient people who were destroyed by natural calamities because of the evil deeds practised by them. It is significant to note that the Qur'an has put the responsibility of causing destruction of civilization upon the shoulders of man himself, instead of ascribing it to mysterious forces of nature. This is evident from the following verses:

ظهر الفساد فى البر والبحر بماكسبت أيدى الناس ليذيقهم بعض الذى عملوا لعلهم يرجعون.

> Corruption doth appear on land and sea because of the evil which men's hands have done, that He (Allah) may make them taste a part of that which they have done, in order that they may return.[7]

وماكان ربك ليهلك القرى بظلم وأهلها مصلحون۔

In truth thy Lord destroyed not the township tyrannously while their folk were doing right.[8]

The above verses clearly show that providential destruction of peoples and their civilization is closely related to man's actions. Faith in, and practice of, these Qur'anic teachings will not only make man virtuous, just and peace-loving, but also guarantee continuous growth of human civilization.

Respect and Courtesy for other Religions

The lack of tolerance and courtesy on the part of one religious community towards the followers of other religions often causes communal disturbances. This also stirs up enmity between nations. But the Qur'an has struck at the very root of this problem by asking its followers not only to tolerate other religions, but also to refrain from showing any disrespect to their religious authorities. Islam recognises and respects prophets of all religions, both known and unknown. Consider, for example, the following verses, in which Muslims have been enjoined to widen their horizon of faith as well as to respect the religious authorities of other religions:

قل آمنا بالله وما أُنزل علينا وما انزل على ابراهيم واسماعيل
واسحاق ويعقوب والأسباط وماأوتى موسىٰ وعيسىٰ
والنبيون من ربهم، لانفرق بين احدمنهم ونحن له مسلمون۔

Say (O Muhammad): We believe in Allah and that which is revealed unto us and that which was revealed unto Abraham and Ismael and Isaac and Jacob and the tribes, and that which was vouchsafed unto Moses and Jesus and the prophets from their

Lord. We make no distinction between any of them, and unto Him we have surrendered.[9]

"وقالوالن يدخل الجنة الامن كان هودا اونصارى تلك امانيهم قل هاتوابرهانكم ان كنتم صادقين. بلى من اسلم وجهه لله وهومحسن فله اجره عندربه ولا خوف عليهم ولاهم يحزنون."

And they say; None entereth paradise unless he be a Jew or a Christian. These are their own desires. Say: Bring your proof (of what ye state) if ye are truthful. Nay, but whosoever surrendereth his purpose to Allah while doing good, his reward is with his Lord; and there shall no fear come upon them neither shall they grieve.[10]

"ان الذين اٰمنوا والذين هادوا والنصارىٰ والصابئين من اٰمن باللـه واليوم الآخروعمل صالحا فلهم اجرهم عندربهم ولاخوف عليهم ولاهم يحزنون".

Lo ! Those who believe [in that which is revealed unto thee, Muhammad] and those who are Jews, and Christians, and Sabeans-whoever believeth in Allah and the Last Day and doeth right surely their reward is with their Lord, and there shall no fear come upon them neither shall they grieve.[11]

ولاتسبوالذين يدعون من دون اللـه فيسبواللـه عدواً بعيرعلم......

> Revile not those unto whom they pray beside Allah lest they wrongfully revile Allah through ignorance...[12]

It is worth mentioning in this context that the Prophet Muhammad himself meted out a kind and gentle treatment to non-Muslims not only in the early years of his prophethood, but also in the later years when he was at the height of his power and at the head of a large army. Numerous instances can be quoted in support of this point. Here it will suffice to mention that the way he treated the delegation of the Christians of Najran has no parallel in the history of other conquerors. He not only played host to them and lodged them in the Prophetic Mosque at Madinah, but also permitted them to offer prayers on Christian lines in the same Mosque.[13]

Formation of Muslim Political Attitude

Islam is basically a unifying and pacific religion. It taught man how to agree to live together in peace and harmony even while disagreeing on religious matters and belonging to different racial stocks and schools of thought. It not only permits Muslims to become full-fledged citizens of a secular nation, but also makes it binding upon them to remain loyal to it as well as to contribute to its welfare, provided it grants freedom of faith to all the constituent communities, and is based on the lofty principles of healthy nationalism. This is in complete agreement with Islamic ethics for political behaviour and cooperation, three main features of which may briefly be mentioned here in order to further illustrate this point.

First, the general Muslim political attitude is governed by their passionate desire to live together and cooperate with others for the welfare of the whole human race on as large a scale as possible. The same idea is conveyed in the following verse:

قل يا اهل الكتاب تعالوا الىٰ كلمة سواء بيننا وبينكم الا نعبدالا الله ولا نشرك به شيئا ولا يتخذ بعضنا بعضاً اربابامن دون الله، فان تولوا فقولوا اشهدوا بانا مسلمون۔

> Say: O people of the scripture! Come to an agreement between us and you that we shall worship none but Allah, and that we shall ascribe no partner unto Him, and that none of us shall take others for lords beside Allah. And if they turn away, then say: Bear witness that we are they who have surrendered unto Him.[14]

Secondly, rightness of purpose and justness of cause are important factors in determining Muslim political behaviour. Therefore, Muslims are prohibited to form any organisation political or otherwise, for the inhuman purpose of committing aggression on any people or for other destructive purpose. This is clearly evident from the following verse:

تعاونوا على البر والتقوىٰ ولاتعاونوا على الاثم والعدوان۔

> But help ye one another unto righteousness and pious duty. Help not one another unto sin and transgression.[15]

Thirdly, with a view to ensuring political stability, Islam attaches the greatest possible sanctity to pacts and agreements made with others. The Prophet Muhammad himself gave a concrete shape to the accommodating political spirit of Islam by concluding a number of pacts and treaties with nonMuslims, namely, the Makkan disbelievers, the Jews, the Christians and Zoroastrians. Of them the treaty signed by him with the Christians of Najran, guaranteeing them protection and freedom of conscience, at a time when Islam had firmly established itself in the Arabian peninsula, is very significant. The English version of this pact, which became a permanent legislation for the treatment of non-Muslim subjects in Islam, is given below:

"To the Christians of Najran and the neighbouring territories, the security of Allah and the pledge of his Prophet are extended for their lives, their religion, and their property – to the present as well as the absent and others besides; there shall be no interference with the practice of their faith or their observances; nor any change in their rights or privileges; no bishop shall be removed from his bishopric; nor any monk from his monastery; nor any priest from his priesthood, and they shall continue to enjoy everything great and small as heretofore; they shall not oppress or be oppressed; they shall not practise the rights of blood-revenge as in the days of ignorance; no tithes shall be levied from them, nor shall they be required to furnish provisions for the troops."[16]

Here it is noteworthy that fulfillment of promises and agreements is one of the essentials of civilisation. It is vital to world peace and social security, as non-fulfillment of them is bound to breed mutual distrust as well as to lead the world to a terrible state of disorder and unrest. A number of Qur'anic verses can be cited in support of this point. A few of them are quoted below:

وأوفوا بعهد الله إذا عاهدتم ولا تنقضوا الأيمان بعد توكيدها......

> Fulfill the covenant of Allah when ye have covenanted, and break not your oaths after the asseveration of them.[17]

وأوفوا بالعهد إن العهد كان مسئولًا۔

> And keep the covenant. Lo ! of the covenant it will be asked.[18]

وإن استنصروكم فى الدين فعليكم النصرالا على قوم بينكم وبينهم ميثاق، والله بما تعملون بصيرٌ۔

> And if they (the Muslims) seek help from you in the matter of religion, then it is your duty to help them except against a folk between whom and you there is a treaty. And Allah is Seer of what ye do.[19]

It is remarkable to note that 'Abdul Rahman 'Azzam, a distinguished Arab scholar and thinker, has maintained in the light of the above verses that the sanctity of a treaty in Islam is above that of religion, as the Islamic law forbids the Muslims to aid their co-religionists against such non-Muslims, with whom they happen to have signed a treaty of peace. In view of this fact it may be asserted that the Muslims are bound by their religion not to betray their respective nations, for their citizenship of a particular nation is based on their will and agreement to remain loyal to it.

Conclusion

In conclusion it may be said that with such a model, accommodating an ethical framework of Islam for peaceful co-existence at their disposal, Muslims need not worry while living even in non-Muslim-dominated pluralistic societies. What they need most is that they should Islamise themselves thoroughly more internally than externally, more in terms of the spirit of Islam and its high ethical standards required and expected of Muslims in their individual and social as well as private and public life. That way they can serve not only as better ambassadors of Islam to the outside world, but also effectively remove the barriers of mutual misunderstanding and unfounded stereotypes about Islam and Muslims that have unfortunately developed through the ages. By doing so they can simultaneously make themselves more lovable, more useful, even indispensable to the spiritually and ethically retarded society at large. Thus, they can convert the position of their being a minority into an opportunity to reassert themselves as servants and friends of Allah by displaying and practising the inherent niceties and beauties of Islam in the light of the essence of its teachings so nicely encapsulated by the Prophet Muhammad as follows:

إنما بعثت لأتمم مكارم الأخلاق.

> I was sent as Prophet to bring to perfection the noble qualities of good behaviour and good character.

References

1. The Qur'an, XLIX : 13 (tr. by M. M.. Pickthall).

2. *Ibid.*, II : 213.

3. Muhammad Qutb, *Islam, the Misunderstood Religion*, pp. 86-87.

4. The Qur'an, XXV, tr. by M. M. Pickthall).

5. *Ibid.*, LVI : 25-26.

6. *Ibid.*, XXV : 63.

7. *Ibid.*, XXX : 4 1.

8. *Ibid.*, XI : 117.

9. *Ibid.*, III : 84.

10. *Ibid.*, II : 111-112.
11. *Ibid.*, II : 62.
12. *Ibid.*, VI : 108.
13. Shibli Nu'mani, *Sirat al-Nabi*, Vol. I, p. 292.
14. The Qur'an, III : 64.
15. *Ibid.*, V : 2.
16. Syed Ameer Ali, *The Spirit of Islam*, p. 272.
17. The Qur'an, XVI : 91 (tr. by M.M. Pickthall).
18. *Ibid.*, XVII : 34.
19. Ibid, VIII : 72.

BIBLIOGRAPHY

Works in Arabic

Ahwani, Ahmad, Fu'ad, 1958 *Ibn Sina*, Egypt.

Ali, Abdul, 1991, *Dirasat fi al-Hadarat al-Islamiyat al-'Arabiyah*, Varanasi : Maktaba Salafia.

'Aqqad, al-, 'Abbas Mahmud, 1956 *Athar al-'Arab fi al-Hadarat al-Awrubbiyah*, Cairo.

'Asqalani, al-, Ibn Hajar, 1330 A.H., *Lisan al-'Arab*, Hyderabad Deccan.

Baghdadi, al-, al-Khatib, 1926, *Al-Tatfil wa Hikayat al-Tufayliyin wa Akhbaruhum*, (ed.) by Kazim al-Muzaffar, Najaf : Al-Maktabah al-Haydariyah.

Baghdadi, al-, al-Khatib, 1964 *Al-Bukhala*, (ed.), by Dr. Ahmad Matlub, Baghdad : Matba 'at al-'Ani.

Baladhuri, al-, Ahmad Bin Yahya, 1956, *Futuh al-Buldan*, Cairo : Maktabat al-Nahdat al-Misriyah.

Beg, Ahmad, 'Isa, n.d., *Tarikh al-Nabat 'ind al-'Arab*, Egypt.

Dasuqi, al-, 'Umar, 1966 *Fi al-Adab al-Hadith*, Beirut : Dar al-Kitab al-'Arabi.

Dayf, Shawqi, n.d., *Al-Fukahah fi Misr*, Cairo : Dar al-Hilal.

Farid, Muhammad Kamil, *Diwan Abi Nuwas*, Cairo.

Farraj, Abdul Sattar Ahmad, n.d., *Akhbar Juha*, Egypt : Maktabah Misr.

Farrukh, 'Umar, 1962, *Tairkh al-Fikr al-'Arabi*, Beirut : Al-Maktab al-Tijari li al-Taba'ah.

Hazm, Ibn, 1992, *Tawq al-Hamamah fi al-Ulfat w-al-Ullaf*, Beirut.

Jabr, Jamil (ed.), 1955 *Nawadir al-Jahiz*, Beirut.

Jahiz, al-, 1958 *Al-Bukhala*, ed. by Taha al-Hajiri, Egypt.

Jawzi, al-, Ibn, n.d., *Akhbar al-Hamqa w-al-Mughaffalin*, Beirut : Al-Maktabat al-Tijariyah.

Kutubi, al-, Muhammad Bin Shakir Bin Ahmad, 1951 *Fawat al-Wafayat*, Cairo : Maktabah Nahdat al-Misriyah.

Mazhar, Jalal, 1960 *Ma'athir al-'Arab 'ala al-Hadarat al-Awrubbiyah*, Cairo : Maktabah al-Anjalu al-Misriyah.

Qalyubi, al-, Ahmad Shihabuddin, 1320 AH *Nawadar al-Qalyubi*, Cairo : Al-Matba 'ah al-'Amirah.

Qayrawani, al-, Abu Ishaq Ibrahim Bin Ali, 1953 *Jam' al-Jawahir fi'l Mulah w-al-Nawadir*, ed. by Ali Muhammad al-Bajawi, Cairo : Dar Ihya al-Kutub.

Qayyim, al-, Ibn, 1950 *Zad al-Ma'ad fi Hadyi Khayr al-'Ibad* (2nd edition), Egypt : Matba'at Mustafa al-Halabi.

Qutaybah, Ibn, n.d., *'Uyun al Akhbar*, Egypt : Tab'at Dar al-Kutub.

Rabbih, Ibn, 'Abd, 1954 *Al-'Iqd al-Farid (Fukahat wa Mulah)*, ed. by Karam al-Bustani, Beirut : Maktabah, Sadir.

Rabbih, Ibn, 1953 *Al-'Iqd al-Farid (al-Majanin w-al-Bukhala w-al-Tufayliyyun)*, ed. by Karam al-Bustani, Beirut : Maktabah, Sadir.

Shabushti, al-, Ali Bin Muhammad, n.d., *Kitab al-Diyarat*, Baghdad : Matba'at al-Ma'arif.

Sharif, Hikmat Beg, n.d., *Nawadir Juha al-Kubra*, Cairo : Al-Maktabah al-Tijariyah, sixth edition.

Shatti, al-, Ahmad Shawkat, n.d., *Al-Tibb 'ind al-'Arab*, Cairo.

Shatti, al-, Shawkat Muwaffaq, 1957, *Tarikh al-Tibb*, Damascus.

Tawhidi, al-, Abu Hayyan, n.d., *Al-Basa'ir w-al-Dhakha'ir*, ed. by Dr. Ibrahim al-Kilani, Damascus.

Tawhidi, al-, Abu Hayyan, n.d., *Al-Imta' w-al-Mu'anasah*, ed. by Dr. Ahmad Amin, Cairo.

Tuqan, Qadri Hafiz, n.d., *Al-'Ulum 'ind al-'Arab*, Cairo : Maktabah Misr.

Usaybi'ah, Ibn Abi, 1882, *'Uyun al-Anba fi Tabaqat al-Atibba*, Egypt : Al-Matba'at al-Wahbiyah.

Yaqut, *Mu'jam al-Buldan*, Vol. XVIII, Egypt.

Works in English

Ahmad, Aziz, 1964 *Studies in Islamic Culture in the Indian Environment*, New Delhi : Oxford University Press.

Ali, Abdul, 1993 *Arab-Islamic Legacy to Life Sciences*, Delhi : Idarah-Adabiyat-i Delli.

Ali, Abdul, 1988 Arab Legacy to Humour Literature, New Delhi : MD Publications.

Ali, Abdul, 1996 *Islamic Dynasties of the Arab East*, New Delhi : M.D. Publications.

Ali, Abdul, 2001 *Eminent Arab-Muslim Medical Scientists*, New Delhi : Kitab Bhavan.

Ameer Ali, Syed, 1978 *The Spirit of Islam*, Delhi : Idarah-i Adabiyat-i Delli, reprint.

Arnold, T.W., 1990 *The Preaching of Islam*, Delhi, reprint.

Bucaille, Maurice, 1978 *The Bible, the Qur'an and Science*, Indianapolis.

Durant, Will, 1963 *The Story of Civilization*, New York : Simon and Schuster.

Farrukh, Umar A., 1954 *The Arab Genius in Science and Philosophy*, tr. from Arabic by John B. Hardie, Washington.

Hayes, John R. (ed.), 1983 *The Genius of Arab Civilization*, London : Eurabia Publishing Ltd., (second edition).

Headley, Lord, 1914 *A Western Awakening to Islam*, London : J.S. Phillips.

Hitti, P.K., 2001 *History of the Arabs*, London : Macmillan Press Ltd., reprint.

Hughes, T.P., 1895 *A Dictionary of Islam*, London.

Husain Athar, 1967 *Prophet Muhammad and His Mission*, Bombay : Asia Publishing House.

Iqbal, Dr. M., 1984 *The Reconstruction of Religious thought in Islam*, New Delhi : Kitab Bhavan, reprint.

Jameelah, Maryam, 1982 *Islam and the Ahl al-Kitab*, Delhi.

Joad, C.E.M., 1946 *The Story of Civilization*, London.

Kamaluddin, Khwaja, 1925, *The Ideal Prophet*, Woking (England).

Khalifa, Mohammad, 1983 *The Sublime Qur'an and Orientalism*, New York : Longman Group Limited.

Koelle, S.W., 1889 *Mohammed and the Rise of Islam*, London : G.P. Putnam's Sons.

Mubarakpuri, Abdul Rahman (ed.), 1352 AH, *The Jami Tirmidhi*, Delhi : Jayyid Barqi Press.

Muir, William, 1858 *Life of Mahomet*, London.

Mulehuddin, Dr., 1986 *Philosophy of Islamic Law and the Orientalists*, New Delhi : Taj Printers, revised edition.

Nadwi, Maulana Abul Hasan, 1979 *Muhammad Rasulullah*, Lucknow : Islamic Research and Publications.

Nicholson, R.A., 1956 *A Literary History of the Arabs*, Cambridge : Cambridge University Press, reprint.

Osler, William, 1922 *The Evolution of Modern Medicine*, New Haven.

Pickthall, M.M., *The Meaning of the Glorious Koran*, New York.

Qutb, Muhammad, 1964 *Islam, the Misunderstood Religion*, Delhi : Board of Islamic Publications.

Radinson, Maxime, 1968 *Mohammed* (tr. by Anne Carter), London : The Penguin Press, revised edition.

Said, Esward W., 1978 *Orientalism*, London.

Shareef, M.M., 1989 *A History of Muslim Philosophy*, Delhi, reprint.

Shaw, G. Bernard, *The Doctor's Dilemma*, ed. by A.C. Ward.

Swartz, Marlin L. (ed.), 1981 *Studies on Islam*, Oxford University Press.

Toynbee, A.J., *A Study of History*, London : Oxford University Press.

Journals

Al-'Arabi, Kuwait, No. 97 (December 1966).

Al-'Arabi, Kuwait, No. 141 (August 1970).

Al-'Arabi, Kuwait, No. 169 (December 1972).

Al-'Arabi, Kuwait, No. 180 (November 1973).

Al-'Arabi, Kuwait, No. 202 (September 1975).

Al-'Arabi, Kuwait, No. 204 (November 1975).

Al-'Arabi, Kuwait, No. 205 (December 1975).

Al-'Arabi, Kuwait, No. 206 (January 1976).

Al-'Arabi, Kuwait, No. 208, (March 1976).

Al-'Arabi, Kuwait, No. 221 (April 1977).

Al-'Arabi, Kuwait, No. 252 (November 1979).

Al-'Arabi, Kuwait, No. 323 (October 1985).

Al-'Arabi, Kuwait, No. 330 (May 1986).

Al-'Arabi, Kuwait, No. 354 (May 1988).

Qafilat al-Zayt, Saudi Arabia (August 1976).

Al-'Ilm, South Africa, Vol. V (January 1985).

Hamdard Islamicus, Pakistan, Vol. VII, No. 2 (1984).

Hamdard Islamicus, Pakistan, Vol. VIII, No. 2 (1985).

Hamdard Medicus, Pakistan, Vol. XXIX, No. 4 (1986).

Hamdard Medicus, Pakistan, Vol. XXX, No. 1 (1987).

The New Arab, Delhi, Vol. V (October 1978).

Islam Today, Morocca, No. 1, 1983.

Muslim World League Journal, Saudi Arabia, Vol. VIII, No. 1 (1981).

Muslim World League Journal, Saudi Arabia, Vol. XVI, Nos. 1&2, (1989).

Encyclopaedias

Al-Mu'jam al-Mufahras li Alfaz al-Qur'an al-Karim, ed. by Muhammad Fu'ad 'Abd al-Baqi, Beirut : Dar Ihya al-Turath al-'Arabi, 1945.

Da'irat al-Ma'arif, ed. by Fu'ad Afram al-Bustani, Beirut : The Catholic Press, 1956-62.

Encyclopaedia Britannica, Vol. XV.

First Encyclopaedia of Islam, Leidin : E.J. Brill, 1986.

Encyclopedia Americana, New York : Americana Corporation, 1966, reprint.

Dictionary of Scientific Biography, New York, 1974.

Urdu Dairah Ma'arif-Islamiyah, Lahore : Danishgah-e-Punjab, 1968.

Lexicons

Al-Munid fi al-Lughah (20th edition), Beirut, The Catholic Press, 1969.

Lisan al-'Arab by Ibn Manzur, Beirut : Dar Beirut, 1955-56.

Arabic-English Dictionary al-Fara'id al-Durriyah, Beirut : The Catholic Press, 1964.

A Modern English-Arabic Dictionary al-Mawrid by Munir Baalabaki, Beirut : Dar al-'Ilm li al-Malayin, 1973.

Student's Standar English-Urdu Dictionary, ed. by Abdul Haq, Delhi : J.S. Sant Singh and Sons, reprint, n.d.

INDEX

A

Abbas, Ali Ibn, 107
Abbasids, 29
Abduh, Muhammad, 176
Abdullah Bin Umar, 77
Abdul Rahman Bin 'Awf, 77, 79
Abraham, 24, 33, 168
Adam, 18, 48, 73, 92
Adudi Hospital, 102
Afghani, al- Jamaluddin, 178
Africa, 30, 66, 116
Ahl al-dhimmah, 30
Ahl al-Kitab, 30
Ahrens, W., 2
Aishah, 9, 65, 130
Akbar, 31
Ali bin Abi Talib, Caliph, 36, 131, 173
Ali, Syed Ameer Ali, 60, 176
Almagest, 122
America, 73, 83
Amin, Ahmad, 134
Anas, 130
Anderson, 4
Ansari, al-, Abu Zayd, 115
Antaki, al-, Dawud, 111
Arabs, 5, 41, 63, 93, 99
Arabian Nights, 5, 6
Aristotle, 10, 46, 71
Armenia, 40
'As, al-, 'Amr Ibn, 131
Ash'ab, 137-139
Ashras, Thumamah Bin, 143
Asma, daughter of Zayd, 164
Asma 'i, al-, Abu Sa'd, 115
Ata, 80
Athenians, 62
'Awwam, al-, Ibn, 115, 117-118
'Ayna, al-, Abu, 137, 140-141
Ayyubi, Salah al-Din, 38
Azzam, 'Abd al-Rahman, 189

B

Babylonians, 70
Bacon, Roger, 120
Badr, 74
Baghdad, 40, 99, 102, 111
Baghdadi, al-, Abdul Latif, 107
Baghdadi, al-, al-Khatib, 135
Bajjah, Ibn, 116
Bakhtishu, Jurjis Ibn, 39
Bakr, Abu, 36, 77, 79-80, 173
Bakri, al-, 10
Baladhuri, al-, 36
Basa'ir, al-w-al-Dhaka'ir, 134
Basel, 104
Battani, al-, 118
Baybars, Zahir, 107
Baytar, al-, Abu Bakr, 113
Baytar, al-, Ibn, 115, 117
Berlin, 99
Bernal, 5
Bilal, 79-80
Biruni, al-, 112m 118, 120-121
Brahmans, 30, 62
Britain, 83, 101
Bucaille, Maurice, 98
Bucer, 62
Buddha, 5
Bukhala, al-, 134, 141
Bukhari, al-, 50
Buran, 53
Burckhardt, 3
Burquq, Sultan, 114

C

Campbell, Harry, 51
Cairo, 99, 102, 113
Carlyle, Thomas, 2
Chamberlen I, Peter, 105
Chauliac, Guy de, 104
China, 40
Chintila, King, 27
Christ, Jesus, 4, 5, 14, 62, 69, 168
Christians, 28, 30, 34, 36, 39-42, 187
Chrystostom, 47
Clausen, J., 84
Colby, F. Moore, 129
Cnut, King, 27
Conder, C.R., 40
Confusius, 5
Constantinopole, 1
Copernicus, Nicolaus, 122
Cordova, 39, 99
Coulson, N?J?, 57
Cremona, 104

D

Damascus, 99, 102
Damdam, Abu, 146
Damiri, al-, Kamaluddin, 112
Dar al-Islam, 40

Darda, al-, Abu, 131
Darwin, 112
Davenport, John, 2
David, 40, 86
Delhi, 20, 176
Denmark, 27, 85
Dhimmis, 30-32, 34, 36-40
Dhu Nuwas, King, 28
Diarmait, King, 62
Dinawari, al-, Abu Hanifah, 115-116
Dorner, A., 57
Dozy, Reinhart, 41
Dulamah, Abu, 150-151

E

Edwards, Robert, 107
Egica, Kinf, 27
Egypt, 1, 101, 105, 113
Egyptians, 70
Euclid, 119
Europe, 40, 83-84, 104, 179
Europeans, 99

F

Farisi, al-, Salman, 79
Fars, 40
Fermat, 119
Filahat, al-, al-Nabatiyah, 117
Firdaws al-Hikmah, 109
Fracastoro, Girilamo, 103
France, 99
Franks, 41
Fraud, 159
Furusiyah, al-, w-al-Khayl, 113

G

Galen, 105
Galilee, 28
Galileo, 118, 121
Gerard, 104
Ghafiqi, al-, 115-116
Ghifari, al-, Abu Basrah, 35
Godfrey, 2
Goldziher, Ignaz, 3, 42
Greece, 3, 42, 48
Greeks, 5, 70-71

H

Hifiz, 23
Hajj, 21, 24-25
Hajjaj, al-, Ibn, 150
Hakim, al-, Fatimid Caliph, 39, 118
Hakim Bin Hazzam, 77
Hamawi, al-, Ya'qub, 10, 135
Hanifah, Imam Abu, 172, 174
Harran, 30
Harvey, William, 107
Hashimi, Al-, Ibn Sakrah, 150
Hawi, al-, 102-103
Hawaiian Islands, 101

Hawqal, 10

Hayat al-Hayawan, 112

Haytham, al-, Ibn, 118-120

Hayyan, Jabir Ibn, 115

Headley, Lord, 14

Hebrews, 40

Heracleus, 31

Hesse, 62

Hibatullah, 111

Higgins, 2

Hims, 31

Hindus, 30, 38, 61

Hira(h), 1, 36

Hisab al-Jabr w-al-Muqabalah, 10

Hisham, 80, 132

Hitti, P.K., 25

Hizam, Muhammad Bin Akhi, 113

Hobbes, 176

Hudud, 165

Humaidah, 53

Hurgronji, C., Snouck, 3

Husain Bin Ali, 53

I

Ibn al-Khatib, Lisanuddin, 103

Ibrahim, Muhammad bin, 150

Idrisi, al-, 10

Ihram, 24

Ijtihad, 8, 168-177

Ikhwan al-Safa (Brethren of Purity), 112

Imran, Ishaq Bin, 109

Imta, al-, w-al-Mu'anasah, 134

India, 40, 42, 46

Indians, 42, 70

Iqbal, Muhammad, 17, 176

'Iqd, al-, al-Farid, 134

Iraq, 40

Ireland, 62

Isaac, 33

Isfahani, Abul Faraj, 149

Isfahani, al-, Abul Qasim, 135

Ishaq, Hunayn Ibn, 107

Ismael, 33

Israel, 40

Istidlal, 171

Istihsan, 172, 174

Italy, 99

I'tifak, 23

'Itq, al-, 75

J

Jacob, 33

Jahangir, 31

Jahiz, al-, 107, 111-112, 134, 140, 149

Jam 'al-Jawahir f-il-Mulah w-al-Nawadir, 134

James I, 105

Jami,al-, li-Mufradat al-Adwiyah, 117
Janadi, al-, Abu, 148
Jannaeus, Alexander, 28
Japan, 83
Jassas, al-, Ibn, 145
Jazzar, al-, Ibn, 110
Jehova, 47
Jerusalem, 37, 78
Jews, 26-27, 30, 33-34, 37, 39-40, 42, 47, 187
Jizyah, 30-32
Joad, C.M., 5
Juha, 135-37
Judariyu, al-, w-al-Hasbah, 103
Judea, 26
Juhani, al-, Abul Qasim, 149

K

Ka'bah, 79
Kamil al-Sina' atayn, 113
Kenya, 66
Kepler, 120
Khadijah, 9, 65, 76
Khalid bin al-Walid, 36
Khaldun, Ibn, 9
Khallal, Abu Bakr, 175
Khallikan, Ibn, 135
Khan, Sayyid Ahmad, 176
Khattab, al-, 'Umar Bin, 36-38, 78-80, 173
Khurdadhbih, Ibn, 9
Khwarizmi, al-, 10, 118
Kifayah, al-, f-il-Tibb, 111
Kitab al-Aghani, 149
Kitab al-Diyarat, 134
Kitab al-Filahah, 118
Kitab al-Hayawan, 111
Kitab al-Nabat, 116
Kitab al-Tajribatayn, 116
Kitab al-Umm, 175
Kitab fi al-Nabat, 116
Kitab Shakl al-Qatta, 121
Kufa, 142, 148
Kulliat, al-, 108
Kushajim, Abu Nasr, 150, 152-153

L

Lamarch, 112
Lamartine, 2
Lammens, 4
Lao-Tse, 5
Leckey, 47
Leipzis, 99
Leonardo, 120
Lincoln, Abraham, 73
Linnaeus, C., 112
Livonia, 27
London, 99
Luther, 62

M

Macdonald, 172

Macdonald, Duncan Black, 3

Madrid, 99

Mahdi, al-Caliph, 143, 150-151

Malik, Imam, 172

Malik, al-, 'Umar Bin, 132

Mamun, al-, Caliph, 53, 144, 148

Mansur, al-, Caliph, 39

Mansuri Hospital, 102

Manu, 47

Maqrizi, al-, 114

Margoliouth, S., 6

Mary, 14

Masalih, al-, al-Mursalah, 172

Masalik al-Absar, 135

Masawayh, Yuhanna Ibn, 107

Massignon, Louis, 3

Mathew, 62

Medina, 77

Mecca, 24, 49, 74, 76-77, 87

Melanchton, 62

Merv, 40

Michelet, 27

Moore, Keith, 107

Morocco, 102

Moses, 33, 168

Mu'adh, 169

Mudawwanah, al-, 175

Mufradat, al-fi Gharib al-Qur'an, 135

Muhadarat al-Udaba, 135

Muhallabi, al-, 149

Muhammad, Prophet, 1-9, 12-16, 19-21, 23, 29, 32-35, 39, 41, 49-50, 54, 59, 63-64, 69-70, 74-78, 80, 87-88, 92-93, 100-101, 129-131, 144, 161, 163-164, 167-168, 170-172, 181, 185, 187, 190

Muhammad, Isma'il bin, 150

Mu'jam al-Buldan, 135

Mukatabah, 75, 77

Mukhassas, al-, 13

Muqni 'at al-Sa'il, 103

Musa, 'Isa bin, 150

Musa, sons of, 118

Muslims, 29-32, 34, 37, 40, 42, 70, 99-101, 108

Mu'tadid, al-, Caliph, 39

Mutawakkil, al-, Caliph, 39

Muttaqi, al-, Caliph, 39

Muwahhidi, Hospital, 102

Muzayyid, 137-140

N

Nadwi, Sayyid Sulayman, 30

Nafi, 80

Nafis, al-, Ibn, 107

Nafs-e-ammarah, 23

Nairobi, 66
Najran, 8, 28, 36, 186
Nasir, al-, 'Abd al-Rahman, 39
Nazareth, 14
Negroes, 25
Netherlands, 83
Nicholson, R.A., 29
Nihayat al-Arab, 135
Noah, 6, 168
Noldeke, 3
Norway, 27
Nu'ayman, 130
Nuremberg, 63
Nuri Hospital, 102
Nuwas, Abu, 137, 139-140
Nuwayri, al-, 112, 135

O

Oxford, 99, 104

P

Padua, 104
Palestine, 28
Paris, 99
Pavlov, 84
Peninsula, Iberian, 26, 28
Persia, 40
Persians, 62
Peter, 14
Pickthall, M.M., 42
Plato, 46, 71
Poll-tax, 31-32
Prussia, 62
Ptolemy, 119
Pumbeditha, 40

Q

Qalawun, Sultan, 113-114
Qanun, al-, (Canon), 110
Qasim, al-, Muhammad bin, 30
Qayrawani, al-, 135
Qayyim, Ibn, 172
Qazwini, al-, Ibn Zakariya, 112
Quff, al-, Ibn, 105
Qutaybah, Ibn, 134

R

Rabbih, Ibn 'Abd, 132, 134
Ramd, 22
Ramadan, 22
Ranke, 3
Rashi,d al-, Harun, 36, 39
Razi, al-, Ibn Zakariya, 102-103, 110
Regiomontanus, 122
Resezwinth, King, 27
Ridwan, Ali Bin, 111
Rigveda, 61
Rodinson, Maxime, 4
Romans, 26, 32, 37, 70

Rome, 3

Romer, 119

Rushd, Ibn, 10, 108, 112

S

Sabeans, 30, 34

Said, Edward, W., 3, 6

Said, Muhammad bin, 146

Salma, Umme, 9, 65

Salim, 80

Servier, Andre, 3

Shabushti, al-, 134

Shadda Bin 'Awf, 87

Shafi'i Imam, 172

Shahadah, 20

Shahjahan, 31

Shahrastani, al-, 29

Shamaqmaq, al-, 150

Shaprut, Hasday Bin, 39

Shaw, George Bernard, 84, 101

Shawkani, al-, Muhammad bin Ali, 176

Shu'aram al-, al-Mujjan, 150

Sidah, Ibn, 113

Sikkit, al-, Ibn, 115

Simeon, 40

Sina, Ibn, 103, 110, 112

Sind, 30

Sizebut, King, 27

Solomon, 62, 86

Spain, 26, 39, 41, 99, 104, 116

Sparta, 46

Spartans, 46

Sukainah, 53

Sura, 40

Suyuti, al-, Jalaluddin, 176

Sweden, 83

Syria, 1, 28, 31

T

Tabari, al-, Ali Ibn Sahl, 103, 109

Tadhkirah fi 'Ilm al-Hay'ah, 122

Tajalli, 20

Taqlid, 176

Tarawih, 23

Tasrif, al-, 104

Tatfil, al-, 135

Tawhidi, al-, Abu Hayyan, 132, 134

Taymiyah, Taqiuddin Ibn, 176

Tertullian, 47

Tha'alibi, al-, 135

Thaqafi, al-, al-Mughirah, 142

Thaqafi, al-, Ghaylan, 63

Tibb, al-, al-Ruhani, 110

Tirmidhi, al-, Muhammad bin Ahmad, 145

Toronto, 107

Torrey, C.C., 2

Toynbee, A.J., 28

Trygvesson, King Olaf, 27
Tulun, Ibn, Hospital, 102
Turkistan, 40
Turkey, 176
Tusi, al-, Nasiruddin, 118, 121-122

U

'Ubaydah, Abu, 31
Uhud, 9, 35, 64-65
'Umar II, 39, 132
'Umari, al-, Ibn Fadlillah, 135
Umayyads, 29
Umdat al-Jarrahin, 105
Umm al-Fazl, 53
Umm al-Habib, 53
Usamah, 80
Uthman, Caliph, 36, 38, 40, 79
Uyun al-Akhbar, 134

V

Venice, 104
Viken, 27
Visigoths, 27-28

W

Wafayat al-A'yan, 135
Wahhab, Muhammad Ibn Abdul, 176
Wahshiyah, Ibn, 115, 117
Walcher, 105
Wali-Allah, Shah, 20, 176
Watt, 4
Westpholia, 63
William Frederick, 62
Witelo, 120
Wollaston, 4

Y

Yatimat al-Dahr, 135
Yemen, 1, 40, 169
Yunus, Ali Bin, 118-119
Yusuf, Abu, 36

Z

Zahrawi, al-, Abul Qasim, 104-105
Zahri, al-, 80
Zajjaj, al-, 145
Zakat, 21, 77
Zangwill, Israel, 41
Zayd Bin Thabit, 80
Zayd, Usamah bin, 131
Zend-Avesta, 62
Zij, al-, al-Hakimi, 119
Zoroastrians, 30, 187
Zubaidah, 53
Zuhr, Ibn, 111
Zuhri, al-, Muhammad Bin Muslim, 132